HAUNTED
PLANO, TEXAS

HAUNTED PLANO, TEXAS

MARY JACOBS

Haunted America

Published by Haunted America
A Division of The History Press
Charleston, SC
www.historypress.com

Front cover: Spirits are rumored to roam the Carpenter House, built in 1898 and located on East Sixteenth Street near downtown Plano. *Photo by the author*; *back cover*: Established in 1847, Baccus Cemetery sits in the middle of busy Legacy Town Center in Plano. *Photo by David Downs, David Downs Photography*; *inset*: Kathy Strobel, a guide at the 2017 Apparition Expedition ghost tour in downtown Plano. *Photo by Debi Adams, Debi Adams Photography*.

First published 2018

Manufactured in the United States

ISBN 9781467140386

Library of Congress Control Number: 2018942447

For Russ Kissick

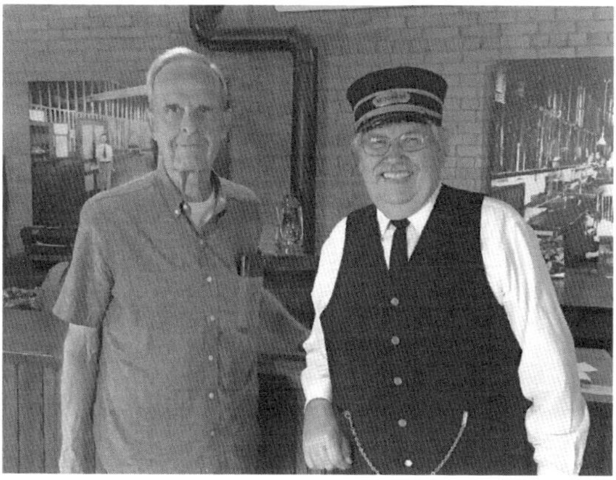

Russ Kissick (*left*) with Harold Larson, president of the Plano Conservancy board. *Photo by the author.*

This book got its start on a sunny September day in 2016. I visited the Interurban Railway Museum to interview Russ Kissick, who shared the story of the Zodiac Rider for an episode of *Plano Podcast*. (It's also in this book, chapter 12.)

I told Russ about my project—collecting "haunted Plano" stories—and he kindly agreed to help. We spent the next few hours strolling the sidewalks of downtown Plano and calling on business owners to ask for their supernatural experiences.

I discovered two things that day: many people had indeed had unexplained experiences. And Russ had an incredible passion for Plano's history. When he learned that young people in Plano had no sense of their roots or of the community's history, he felt he had to do something. So, Russ helped start a museum. Then he spent years as a volunteer, telling schoolchildren about Plano's past.

Sadly, Russ passed away less than a year later. But his generous and kind spirit is still with us, and I like to think it will continue to haunt Plano for many years to come.

CONTENTS

PREFACE

Do you believe in ghosts?

I won't try to convince you of the reality of the paranormal, because I'm not convinced myself. But I will tell you a story.

Many years ago, while working late on a writing project, I was stumped. The words just wouldn't flow. Finally, I gave up and went to bed and dreamed of my former boss, Clint, who had passed away a few months earlier. He was a great editor and mentor and a creative soul who wrote plays in his spare time.

In the dream, he showed up unannounced at my front door. I was mortified. "I thought you were dead," I confessed with embarrassment. Clint grinned, shrugged his shoulders nonchalantly and said, "Nah, I'm not."

The next day, returning to the writing project, the words immediately flowed. A friend theorized that the ghost of Clint had given me his muse.

Did my departed boss literally emerge from the afterlife to bestow his creative gifts on me? Or did the dream simply reawaken memories of the sense of creative joy absorbed while working with Clint? And did it really matter? Aren't both scenarios equally miraculous? When someone lives on in our memory and imagination, still inspiring and guiding us, isn't that wondrous?

So that's my view of ghost stories. Maybe there's some residual energy of long dead souls that still permeates the walls of old buildings, and we haven't yet figured out how to measure it. Or maybe ghosts simply exist in our memories and imaginations, triggered when we spend time in places filled with history. The question "Which is it?" seems moot.

During the holiday season, we might sing "Santa Claus Is Coming to Town" or wave at Santa in a Christmas parade, even if we don't believe there's a guy in a red suit living at the North Pole. But the most devout disbelievers might allow that, through the spirit of generous souls, Santa is real.

I invite you to approach these stories in the same spirit. Suspend your disbelief a bit, enjoy the brief shiver of delicious terror that comes with pondering the possibility that spirits still walk among us, and while you do, connect with Plano's fascinating history.

ACKNOWLEDGEMENTS

No woman is an island, and no book gets written in solitude, especially not a history book. I would like to thank all those who took time to speak to me, to share their ghost stories and to assist me in tracking down the photos and information I needed.

Anyone interested in local history knows that the Genealogy Center at the Plano Public Library is a Plano treasure. Genealogy librarian Cheryl Smith's help on this and other history projects has been invaluable.

Jennifer Shertzer, Debi Adams and David Downs kindly shared many of the beautiful photos you'll see in this book.

Over breakfast at IHOP, Kenny Bush shared a wealth of spooky stories from the 1960s and 1970s and patiently helped me check facts.

Another gold mine was the Plano History (the Early Years) Facebook page, ably administered by John Brooks.

Others whose assistance and input were much appreciated include: Jamey Jamison, Michael Hamilton, Sam Hodges, Tammy Hooker, Leesie Pool, Michael Whitehead, Gwen Workman, Kathy Strobel, Joy Gough, Candace Fountoulakis, Charlotte Carpenter Johnson, Debbie Holman, Connor Chaddick, Detective Luke Grant of the Plano Police Department, Janice Cline, André Davidson, Brad Jones, Kevin Main, Bob Pannell, Michelle Hawkins, Steve Sims and all the lovely folks at the Plano Conservancy for Historic Preservation, including Jeff Campbell, Jessica Woods, Charlotte Loontiens and Jack Durnin.

Finally, my deepest gratitude goes to my dear husband, Steve Lavine. Without his support, insights and Photoshop skills, this never would've gotten done.

1

THE HAUNTED CITY

If you look long into the dark
Something will illuminate or spark
If you wade where the silence is deep
If you listen long enough it speaks

—lyrics from Haunted, *by Carrie Newcomer*

What haunts a city? In researching this book, I was surprised how many people in Plano believe they live or work in buildings that are haunted. They have some great stories, and I had a blast collecting them.

But through my research, I realized that there are many ways that a city may be haunted. They don't all involve supernatural apparitions.

A city may be haunted by what it once was. Around 1950, Plano's farming community watched in dismay as the city morphed into a bedroom community. People who grew up in Plano in the 1960s and 1970s are wistful for the days when it was a small town. Others who arrived in the 1980s and 1990s miss the time when Plano was just a suburb, when homes were relatively inexpensive and the roads were less congested.

All of which makes me wonder: What will make us look back on 2018 with nostalgia? What if, to quote Carly Simon, these *are* the good old days?

Fears haunt a city's psyche. The pioneers of Plano faced real and incredibly frightening threats: Indian attacks, smallpox, crop failure. Life

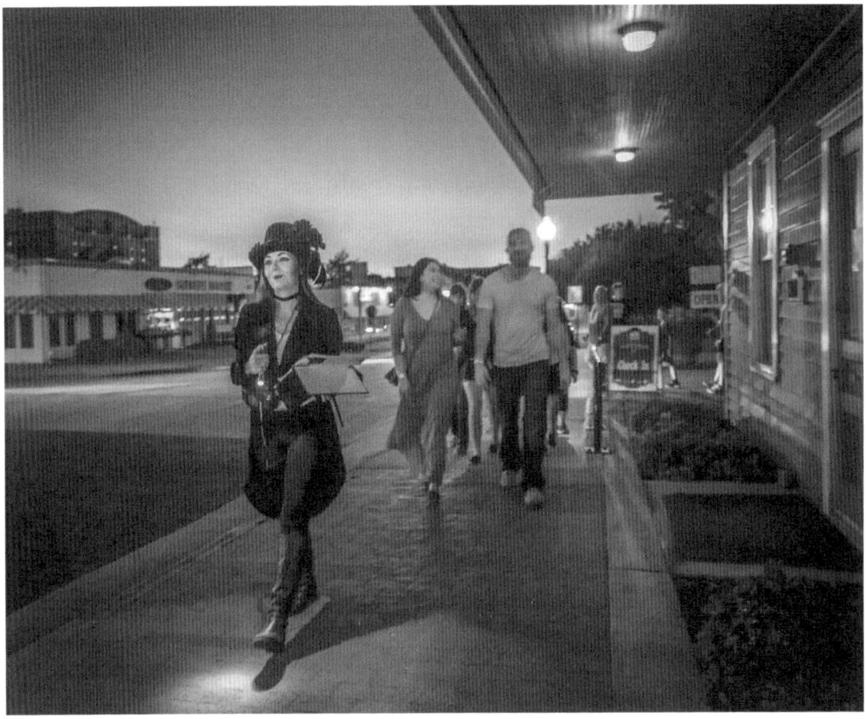

Tammy Hooker leads a group of ghost tourists at the 2017 Apparition Expedition in downtown Plano. *Photo by Jennifer Shertzer.*

was hard and uncertain. And yet these pioneers persisted and built lives, families and prosperous businesses. But waves of unsubstantiated fear can also tear through a community, expand and take a life of their own—without much factual basis. I've lived through a few of them myself: the Satanic Panic of the 1980s, and the Clown Threat that terrorized America for all of about two weeks in 2016. Writing this book, I pondered the grip our fears have on us, even when there's little credible evidence to justify them. (Although one Plano man's 2016 encounter with a baseball bat–wielding clown *was* truly scary.)

A city is also haunted by its tragedies. Those of distant memory become hair-raising tales to share around a campfire. More recent tragedies are too raw to inspire ghost stories. Those haunt us in Plano, too. I saw that while interviewing people who experienced Plano's heroin epidemic of the 1990s. Take the hardboiled detective whose voice still cracks with emotion as he describes finding the body of a young man, killed by an overdose. Or the counselor who works with people who got hooked in the 1990s and still struggle with addiction today. Heroin took a terrible toll on our community. It still haunts us.

So why write a book called *Haunted Plano*? Our haunted history reveals some common threads that speak to us today. Over the years, the people of Plano have responded to daunting challenges with determination, initiative and cooperation. When multiple fires destroyed downtown Plano, the city organized the fire department, which ultimately became one of the best-equipped, most highly trained in the country. When smallpox rocked the community, city council initiated a quarantine and a program of vaccination. When kids began dying of heroin overdoses, city leaders called a community meeting at Plano Centre, hoping to attract a few dozen concerned parents. Instead, cars lined up for miles along Spring Creek Parkway, and the auditorium was standing room only. The response by Plano's leaders and law enforcement remains a model for other cities to this day.

When dark moments strike, Plano citizens have a history of rolling up their sleeves and getting to work, together. That's why Plano has been down, but never out. May we remember that as we tackle whatever challenges lay ahead.

A BRIEF HISTORY OF PLANO

Author's Note: To really appreciate our haunted history, you need an overview of the city's history and development. I offer this short version of Plano's past, with a nod to the ghost stories relating to each key period of time.

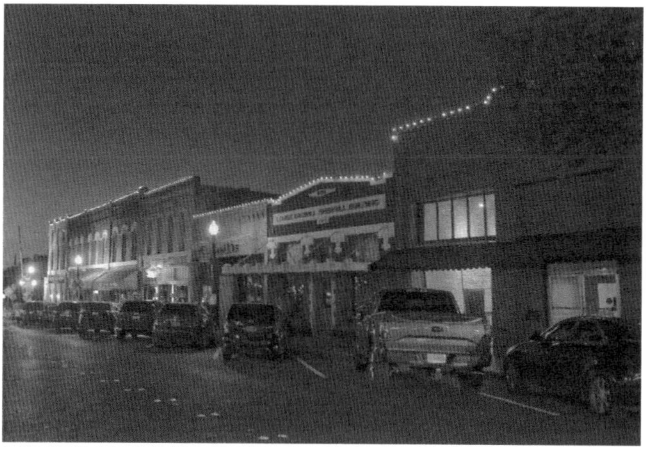

Downtown Plano, October 2017. *Photo by Debi Adams.*

EARLY SETTLERS (1842–72)

Population, 1870: 155

Opportunity brings people to Plano from around the world. It's true today, and it was true in the city's earliest days. For Plano's first settlers, that opportunity came in the form of land.

In 1841, the Republic of Texas was in financial straits, and its "very existence depended on attracting people to settle the vast expanse of land."[1] The Republic contracted with twenty men to start the Peters Colony in North Texas in exchange for free land. A married man received 640 acres; a single man got 320 acres. Settlers were expected to live on the land for three years, build a cabin and fence and cultivate at least 15 acres. The area that's now Plano was particularly attractive to farmers because it offered "the best and richest blackland in North Texas and was thought by many to be the best in the United States."[2]

Life was hard on the frontier. Settlers were spaced far apart. The threat of Indian raids always loomed, especially after "The Muncey Incident" in 1844. Gradually, a community emerged, and by 1850, the Plano area had its first school, its first cemetery and a Methodist class, the beginnings of what today is First United Methodist Church of Plano.

William Forman I became the first official postmaster, and the name Plano was established. Forman's son built the oldest house still occupied in Plano today; evidence of its original owners may linger in the form of a mysterious aroma, as told in "The Uncanny Cook." Collin County established its own law enforcement, and a Plano man played a key role in the sensational trial of a teenaged con man that led to "The Hanging of Stephen Ballew."

The Civil War (1861–65) brought growth to a standstill in Plano. Union sentiments were strong, because most settlers had come from the upper South—Kentucky and Tennessee—leading Collin County to become one of the few counties in the state to oppose secession. The settlers had relatively few slaves, and as a result, "Collin County developed with more of a Midwestern culture than a southern one, which meant that the area had more artisans and professionals."[3]

Postwar Prosperity (1872–1900)

Population, 1900: 1,304

With the arrival of the railroad linking McKinney and Dallas in 1872, life changed dramatically in Plano. Downtown became the prosperous center of a booming farm economy, thanks to the emergence of cotton as a cash crop, cheap fencing in the form of barbed wire and the development of mechanized farm equipment. The city was incorporated in 1873.

Congregations built churches, and proprietors opened businesses downtown. City leaders established a public school system, with the first high school class graduating in 1892. The mayor's office, city council and city court were also established in 1881, meeting the first and third Tuesdays of each month in the back of a saddlery shop.

Fires plagued the downtown area, destroying multiple buildings downtown in 1881, 1889, 1895 and again in 1897. City leaders responded by establishing a fire department and building a water system. Many of the downtown businesses and homes still have wells created during this time period. Read about the wells still there in many downtown buildings in "What Lurks Beneath."

One important Plano institution, the Masonic Lodge, re-chartered in 1894. The Lodge played a key role in Plano's civic life and remains active today, meeting in what may be the most haunted building in Plano. Read about it in "The Masonic Lodge."

Medical care on the frontier was limited, and death was a part of daily life, as you'll see in the chapters "Plano's Darkest Hour" and "Death in Early Plano." Childhood disease killed many children, possibly including Edna Bowman, who died at age six in 1885. Her tombstone inspired an urban legend that still circulates today, described in the chapter "Edna, the Bad Seed?"

Plano's leading citizens loved to entertain and built beautiful homes, some of which are still standing and believed to be haunted. See their stories in the chapters "The Phantom Pianist," "The Spooky Spinster," "Heritage Farm Hauntings" and "The Paranormal Playmate." Another tale, "The Murdered Dentist," originates in a building erected in the downtown business district during this time.

Small-Town Plano (1900–50)

Population, 1950: 2,126

In the first half of the twentieth century, Plano transitioned from a frontier community into a small but forward-looking town. By the mid-1900s, the annual Old Settlers Reunion Picnic and Barbecue faded away as the city's original settlers died.

During this time, city leaders led the establishment of a modern infrastructure—electricity and telephone service, trash collection, a sewer system, as well as parcel post, air mail and door-to-door mail service. By 1925, Plano was one of the first towns of its size in Texas with paved streets.

In 1908, the Texas Electric Railway began service that linked Denison and Dallas by way of Plano. That brought commerce to Plano as well as crime. The city had only two law enforcement officers, one of whom became Plano's first fallen police officer in 1920—and for many years, the only one. Read the story of Green Wesley Rye, "The Night Watchman."

Churches were the center of social life and strongly influenced Plano's culture. In 1902, the community resoundingly voted liquor and saloons out of Plano and kept them out for the next eighty years. Blue laws kept businesses shuttered on Sundays.

Schools and civic organizations also flourished during this time. By 1913, Plano High School had organized football and baseball teams; in 1925, the Plano Wildcats celebrated their first undefeated season. The Cox Building was built to serve all white Plano schoolchildren; today, some folks in the building believe one of those youngsters still haunts the halls, "The Giggling Ghost." Also built in 1917 was the Saigling House, now the ArtCentre of Plano, home of a grumpy ghoul we call "The Haughty Hostess."

As the economy boomed after World War II, cars became more affordable, quickly displacing railways as the main source of transportation and leading to the close of the interurban railway in 1948. That likely ended the career of "The Zodiac Rider," but some say she's still around.

Around the same time, developers began buying farm land in Plano and surrounding areas. By 1950, Plano was on the verge of another period of great change.

Growing Bedroom Community (1950–80)

Population, 1980: 72,330

Plano's years as a farming-based economy came to a close around 1950, with the arrival of small industry and the reappraisal of land values for tax purposes.

Probably the single-most important factor contributing to Plano's growth was the extension of North Central Expressway from Campbell Road to Plano in 1957. Plano became a prime destination for people who worked in Dallas but wanted to live in a more suburban environment. By 1960, Plano had become the fastest-growing city in Collin County.

Ahead of other cities in North Texas, Plano ISD voluntarily initiated desegregation in the 1964–65 school year at Plano High. Athletics helped unite the Anglo and African American communities, as the Plano High School Wildcats captured a state championship in football in 1965.

New subdivisions began to crop up like mushrooms; schools and libraries were added to meet the growing demand. In 1970, Herbert Hunt announced plans for a new $500 million, 3,959-acre business and residential development in North Texas, with the majority of the property falling within the city limits of Plano.

Those who grew up in Plano during these days have fond memories of holidays in Plano—see the chapter on "Halloween Hijinks"—as well as Plano's own Boo Radley–like character, "The Witch Lady of Plano." Urban legends surrounding "The Goat Man" and "Stranger Things at Ranch 111" inspired scary outings for thrill-seeking teens.

In 1979, Ross Perot announced that Electronic Data Systems (EDS) had purchased nearly two thousand acres of land, signaling its plans to relocate corporate headquarters to Plano and the beginnings of the Legacy Business Park. As the 1980s dawned, big change was on the horizon.

Explosive Growth (1980–2000)

Population, 2000: 222,030

The last two decades of the twentieth century saw explosive growth in Plano, with EDS, Frito-Lay, JCPenney and other large companies moving their headquarters here. Plano's population exploded, transforming a bedroom community to a large city. Collin Creek Mall opened in 1981. In 1995, the President George Bush Highway opened, providing an east–west connection across Plano. Another major road, the North Dallas Tollway, extended into Plano, connecting the west side to Dallas.

As the population grew, so did Plano ISD. In 1980, the system had more than twenty-two thousand students, and seventeen elementary schools, five middle schools and three high schools; many more school buildings were added in the next twenty years.

All this explosive growth had a dark side. Fourteen Plano teenagers committed suicide from 1983 to 1984. Between 1996 and 1997, eleven young people in Plano died of heroin overdoses. Both episodes thrust the city into the national spotlight, portraying Plano as a poster city for suburban dystopia.

With the heroin epidemic, the community mobilized to educate teens and law enforcement went after the dealers. Near the end of 1997, Plano police announced the arrest of the city's biggest heroin supplier.

In the late 1990s, with construction for the DART light commuter rail underway, downtown Plano began to enjoy a renaissance. Michael Hamilton was one of the people drawn to the historic area; his story of "The Lonely Widow" will send a chill up your spine.

RECENT YEARS (2000–PRESENT)

Population, 2016 (estimated): 286,057

Recent years have brought continued, major growth in Plano, with the arrival of corporate and regional headquarters for Toyota, FedEx Office, Liberty Mutual, JP Morgan Chase and Boeing. Legacy Town Center added shops and restaurants, followed by development of Legacy West. DART light rail service opened in Plano in 2002, accelerating the renaissance of downtown.

Plano not only witnessed massive growth in population but also significant changes in demographics. The arrival of corporate headquarters brought professionals from around the world and boosted the city's diversity. In 1980, Plano was more than 90 percent Anglo; by the 2010 census, about 55 percent of Plano's population was Anglo, 19 percent Asian, 8 percent African American and 15 percent Hispanic.

Through all these changes, a committed group of Plano citizens worked diligently to preserve Plano's history, haunted or otherwise. The Plano Conservancy for Historic Preservation was established in 2001, and the Interurban Museum opened in 2003. Read the stories of Plano's passionate history advocates in "Keepers of the Family Plots," "Tombstone Mysteries" and "Who Ya Gonna Call?"

Some Plano residents still encounter ghosts from time to time, like the 2009 story of "The Evaporating Apparition," the recent sightings in "Ghosts around Town" and the non-supernatural, but still scary, "Clown Threat" of 2016.

II

GHOST SIGHTINGS

1

The Masonic Lodge

Plano's Most Haunted Building

There was no doubt in his mind. Kevin Main was absolutely certain he had locked the door.

Kevin was working late, alone, well into the night, preparing a meal that the brothers would share the following evening. He always made sure the door was secure before going upstairs to work in the second-floor kitchen late at night. Given the Masonic Lodge's downtown location, confused passersby occasionally wandered in if the door was left unlocked.

So, there was no explanation when he heard the sound of footsteps on the stairs. Heavy, deliberate footsteps, like a man wearing work boots.

A chill went up Kevin's spine as he peered down the stairwell. No one was there.

Other Hauntings

Kevin Main's experience was one of many reported by the members of Plano Masonic Lodge No. 768, AF & AM, which could easily be Plano's most haunted old building.

"That happened a number of times, and I'm not the only one who has heard it," he said. "Many brothers working here late have heard these footsteps on the stairs."

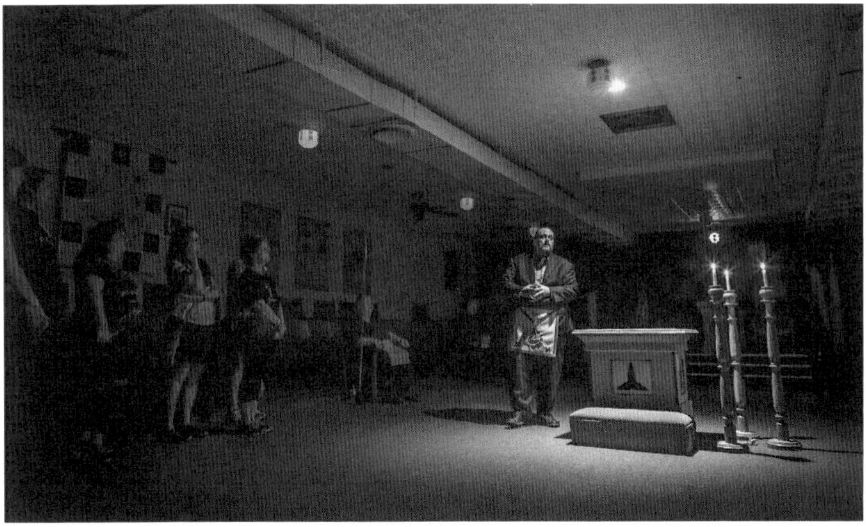

Kevin Main speaks to visitors in the Masonic Lodge during the Apparition Expedition ghost tour, October 2017. *Photo by Jennifer Shertzer.*

On another occasion, Kevin remembered descending the stairwell, and just as he reached the landing, about halfway down, he heard footsteps right behind him.

"This was years ago, and I don't remember anything else from that evening, but the footsteps—they were so clear," he recalled.

Spooky Seats

If you're not a Mason, you'll need special permission to enter the main room where the Lodge meetings take place. There you'll see a candlelit altar, an original pressed-tin ceiling and a lighted letter *G*, which stands for "God" and "Geometry." There's a wall of portraits of the Lodge's past masters, most of them long dead, peering over the proceedings. Theater-style chairs line each side of the room, with seats that may be raised or lowered as needed.

On many occasions, a brother has arrived at the building, alone, and peeked inside the main room, noticing that three or four seats were in the down position. A little later, he'd return and see those same seats in the raised position.

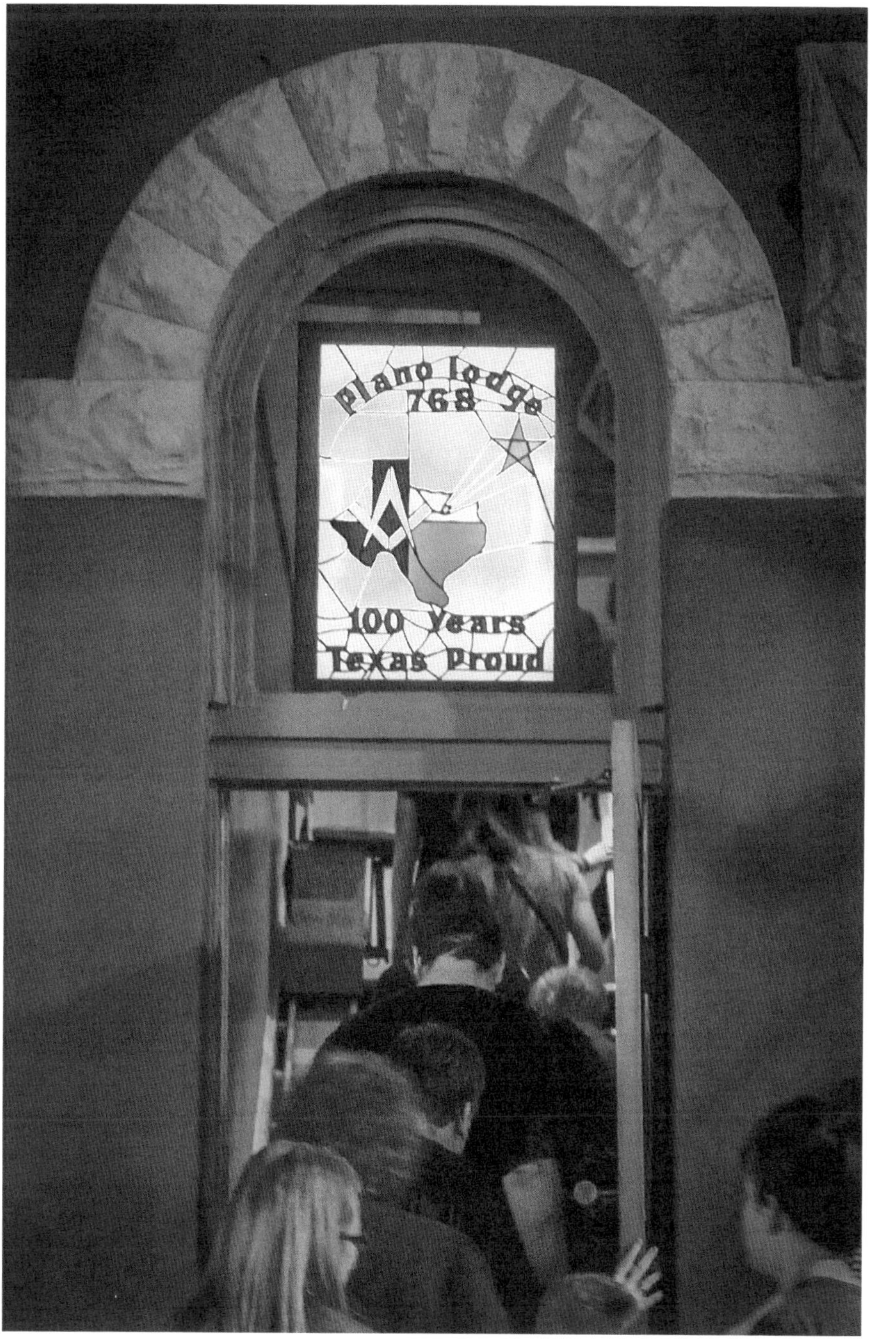

The *G* stands for God and Geometry. *Photo by Jennifer Shertzer.*

It's happened more than once to Kevin Main.

"I would've known if someone was in the building at the time, but there wasn't," he said. "This was a common experience, something many others have witnessed as well."

One past master of the Lodge has heard the sound of a little girl laughing late at night. He was so unnerved that he no longer enters the building alone after dark. One woman was frightened by the same sound more than thirty years ago while leading meetings of Rainbow Girls (an associated group for young girls).

On other occasions, Kevin witnessed doors closing on their own and objects moving with no human involvement, like the chair that slid out from under a table and across the floor.

Years ago, two paranormal investigation teams spent the night in the building, with Kevin there to supervise. They spotted orbs and other signs of paranormal activity.

"One woman in particular pointed to the pictures of past members on the wall, and she was confirming some things about these men that would not be common knowledge," he said.

The Masonic Spirit

Kevin Main attributes the sounds of footsteps to the spirit of J.W. Shepard, one of the building's early owners and a Mason himself.

"The footsteps on the stairs feel like a strong presence—someone who's self-assured, confident and maybe not very happy," Kevin said. "In my mind, I've always connected the unexplained happenings to Shepard."

Shepard owned a 2,200-acre cattle ranch and farm in Plano and was internationally known for his fine livestock, especially his mules. He also owned eleven cotton gins, a cottonseed oil mill and a flour mill. Shepard served on Plano ISD's school board from 1899 until 1911 and on the Plano City Council.

When Shepard passed away in 1946, his obituary in the *Dallas Morning News* said, "Probably no other man has done so much for Plano and south Collin County, furnished work to more people and fed more hungry, less fortunate people, than J.W. Shepard."[4]

Shepard and his wife sold the building to the Masonic Lodge No. 768 in 1924. Maybe he doesn't care for the intrusion. Or possibly, as a Mason and a

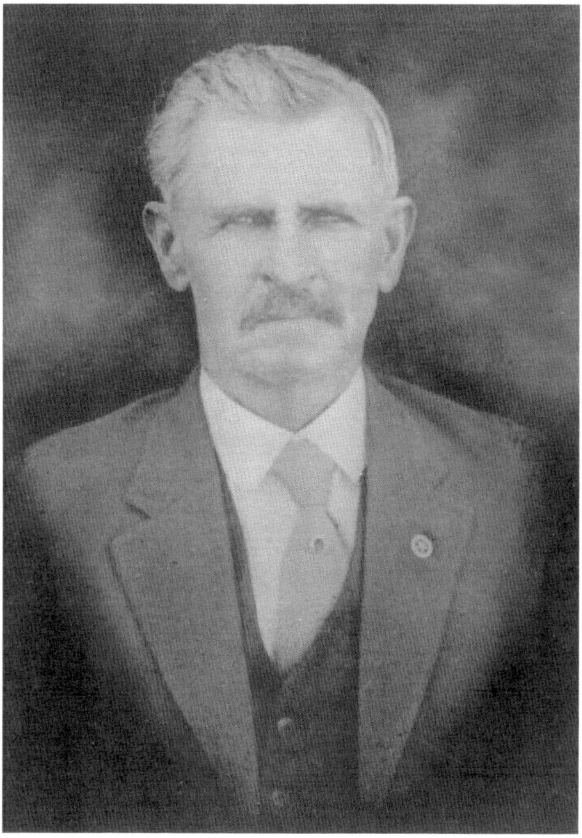

Does J.W. Shepard still haunt the halls of the Masonic Lodge? *From the Frances Bates Wells Collection, courtesy of the Genealogy Center, Plano Public Library.*

member of the Lodge, Shepard just wants to make his presence known. J.W. Shepard was an influential citizen and an important figure in Plano's history. Maybe he just can't quite let go of his beloved hometown.

Look at a photo of Shepard, and you might agree with Kevin's theory. Shepard stares back with an unrelenting gaze. You do get a sense of an imposing and powerful person who might just be too stubborn to let death keep him down.

Founding Fathers

The building that's now home to Masonic Lodge No. 768 was once the location of one of Plano's first hotels, the Moore House. Travelers passing through on the Houston and Texas Central Railroad, just a few steps away,

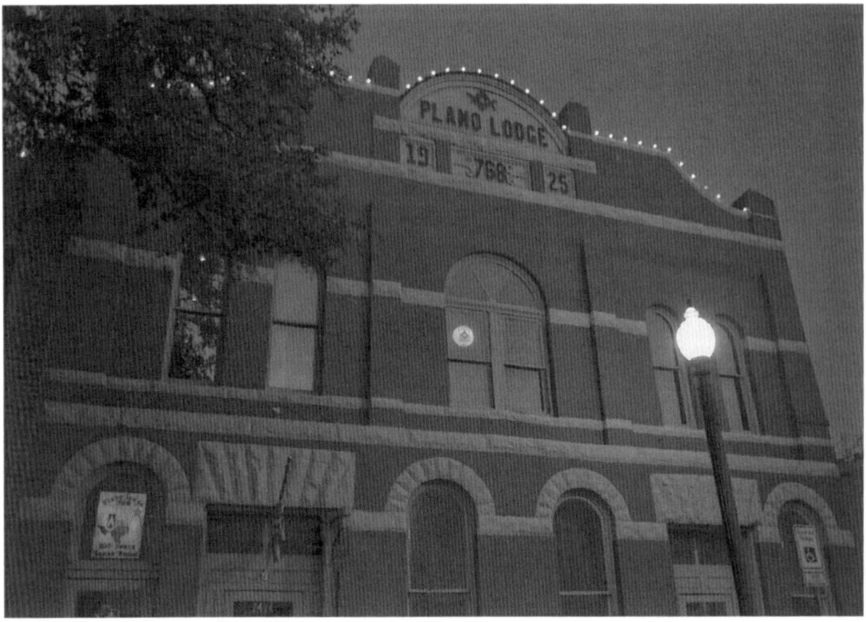

Exterior of the Masonic Lodge. *Photo by Debi Adams.*

would stay here. The original Moore House burned down in the great fire of 1895, along with much of downtown Plano. The brick building that's now standing replaced it a few years later.

As you enter the building, notice the numbers on the façade: 19, 768, 25. Those represent the year the Masons finished remodeling the building and began occupying it—1925—and the Lodge's number, 768. So that's why it says "1925" even though it was built almost thirty years earlier. It's one of the oldest buildings in the downtown area.

On the first floor, there's a Masonic museum that's open to the public on Monday, Wednesday and Friday afternoons.

Many of the men who helped build Plano were also members of Lodge No. 768, and the Lodge's history is closely intertwined with the city's history. The portraits of past masters lining the wall of the meeting room bear familiar Plano names: Hughston, Gulledge, Vines, Sigler and Robinson, all of whom have Plano ISD schools named after them or their family members. Other past Lodge members who also have Plano ISD schools as namesakes: Aldridge, Christie, Daffron, Forman, Haggard, Jasper, Shepard and Weatherford. Past members include about a dozen Plano mayors and about forty who were members of Plano's city council.

Oldest Fraternity

Freemasonry is the world's oldest and largest fraternity, with its past membership including the likes of Benjamin Franklin, Franklin Roosevelt, George Washington, Mozart, Davy Crockett, Henry Houdini and, yes, even Colonel Sanders.

Freemasonry began in medieval Europe as a guild for stonemasons; now, it's a social organization that calls on the tools and concepts of stonemasonry to teach key principles. Just as stonemasons followed certain techniques to construct buildings that remained strong and upright, the Masons' principles offer practical instruction about how to get through life. For example, a stonemason used a level, a symbol that represents equality, justice, fairness and equity. Masons may speak of "the plum line of righteousness" or of creating a cornerstone, a philosophical grounding that allows one "to stand upright before men."

The Plano Lodge, which will celebrate its 125th year in 2019, currently counts about 250 brothers in its membership.

The Lodge's fellowship has brought together people who might not otherwise have met. The membership has counted Jews, Muslims, Hindus and Buddhists as well as Catholic and Protestant Christians in its rolls. It's not a religion or a secret society—as longtime Plano Lodge member Bob Pannell likes to say, paraphrasing Ben Franklin, "The only secret in Masonry is, we have no secrets."

To become a member, one must petition the Lodge, demonstrate good character and profess a belief in a supreme being.

The Masonic Spirits

So why is the Masonic Lodge so haunted? The ancient Celts used the term "thin places" to describe places where the veil between this life and the next is thin.

Masons spend a lot of time pondering this life as well as the next. To become a Mason, you must go through three degrees, representing the three main phases of life—youth, manhood and, finally, old age and death. (And yes, that's where the expression "the third degree" originates.)

It's not morbid—it's a reflection on the briefness of our earthly existence and the importance of living well during our short time in this

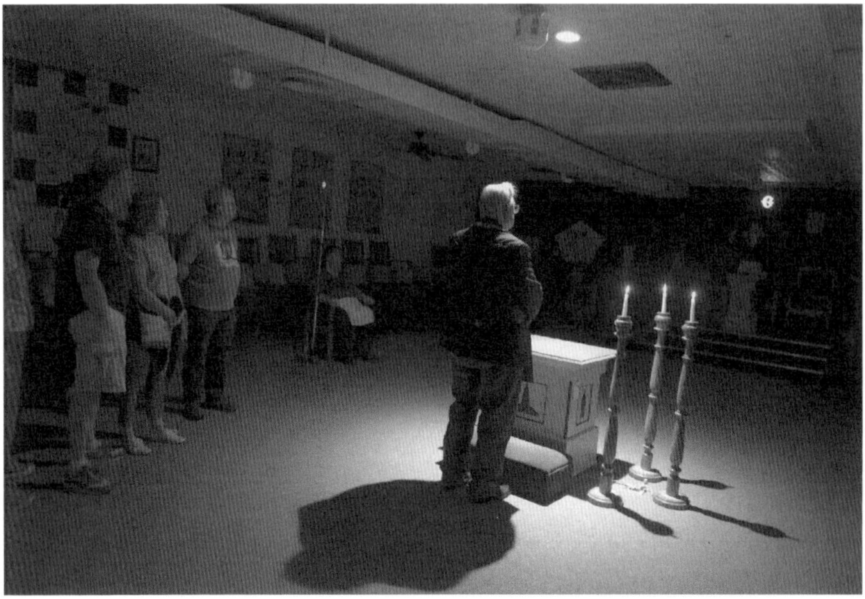

Bob Pannell introduces guests in the Lodge's main meeting room during Apparition Expedition, October 2017. *Photo by Debi Adams.*

realm. While it's not a religious organization, Masons do believe in the immortality of the soul.

Maybe that's what makes this Masonic Lodge—a thin place—a space where the spirits feel at home? It's something to ponder.

2

The Evaporating Apparition

There's probably a rational explanation for most of the strange happenings in the Art Centre Theatre's former downtown location. Sure, the place was a little odd and eerie. Sure, the building had a colorful history. It was old and creaky and, in the summer, unbearably hot.

But Jamey Jamison, the Art Centre Theatre's executive director, can't explain what he saw one day in August 2009.

The theater was located behind the Art Centre of Plano, then at the corner of Fifteenth Street and Avenue K. Today, Shinola occupies the main building; the back building that once housed the theater has since been demolished. Many years before, the building housed the E.O. Harrington Furniture and Undertaking Company.

"The space we occupied was filled with nooks and crannies and hidey holes," Jamey said. "There were cubbies located twenty feet off the floor that had no apparent purpose other than to be creepy."

The storage area was under the seating area; staff members had to crawl into a black void under the seats, as Jamey puts it, "with nothing but a flashlight and your wits to find things." The offices were upstairs above the stage and had access to an attic, which also had no lighting and was very tight.

"Over time, we learned that the building had a colorful history," said Jamey. "It's been used as a storage facility for a mortuary, a furniture store and other things for which we could never find official records." Similarly, there were rumors that a woman had died just outside the building, but no one could corroborate that story.

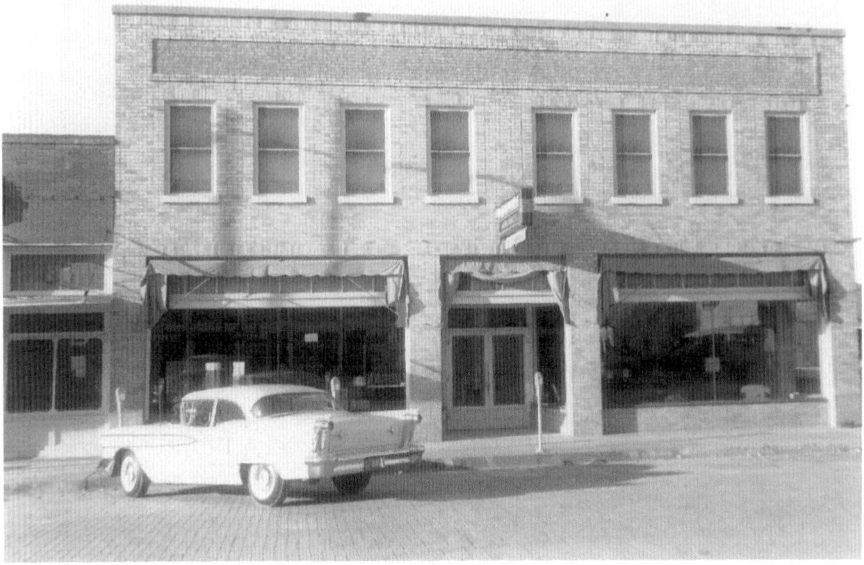

Over the years, many different businesses have occupied the building that's now home to Shinola. Downtown Plano, 1958. *Courtesy of the Genealogy Center, Plano Public Library.*

On top of all that, the Art Centre Theatre was unbearably hot in the summers.

"We cannot attribute everything we saw to ghosts—some may have been heat-induced hallucinations," he said. Basically, the building was a huge metal warehouse with little or no insulation. The roof was not sealed, to allow ventilation in some parts of the building, so staff could hear and sometimes see outside.

To compound the creepiness, downtown had a rat problem at the time. "It was so bad that on trash day when the businesses would take out the trash there was literally a line of rats on the rooftops of both sides of the alleyways waiting for you to leave so they could ravage the trash cans," he recalled.

The theater's back door was tricky and sometimes did not shut. Homeless people occasionally snuck in to sleep in the dressing rooms, which, Jamey said, "would often scare the beejesus out of me."

GHOSTLY VISITATION

But all that can be explained, Jamey said—with the exception of one frightening encounter.

To appreciate this story, you have to understand that the theater's tech booth—where lighting and audio are controlled from a board during performances—was located at the top of the building above the back row, removed from the rest of the building. There was only one way up or down, through a narrow staircase that seemed to rise up backward as you ascended.

When the ghostly visitation took place, only two people were in the building, Jamey and his business partner, Angela Montgomery. They were working on lights for the stage and programming them into the system for an upcoming production. Jamey was in the tech booth; because it was August, he kept all the lights off to help keep it just a little cooler. Angela was working on the stage, about two hundred feet away and thirty feet below the tech booth.

At one point, Angela left the stage to fetch an item she needed. She told Jamey she'd be right back.

"A few moments later, I felt something beside the right side of my head, which was the side of the room toward the entrance of the booth," he said. "I glanced just briefly in that direction and saw a woman."

Because the room was dimly lit, and because he had just looked long enough to register her face, Jamey assumed it was Angela. Unfazed, he continued working.

"The presence was there the way it is when you *feel* someone behind you or beside you, and there was a warmth—not cold but warmth," he said. "In August, that was distinct because it was already significantly warm in the booth."

Thinking Angela was in the room, Jamey said he'd be done in two minutes and then they could go get lunch. At the very same moment, he saw Angela walk back onto the stage.

"I turned just in time to see whatever this was evaporate and rise into the ceiling," he said. "Which was odd, because the only thing above that room is the roof." There was no room above, nothing for the apparition to evaporate into.

"I literally climbed through the window and down into the audience seating area to get away," Jamey said.

He and Angela searched the building thoroughly. All doors were locked. There were no windows to the outside, and no one else had been in the theater all day. From then on, no matter how hot the weather, Jamey never again worked in the tech room without all the lights on.

Jamey has no idea what he saw or how the apparition might connect with the building's history, but she brought to mind the floating female specter in the film *The Abyss*.

"No clue," he said. "She was very pale and blonde…and had a shape but not a form."

A few years later, the Art Centre Theatre moved to 5220 Village Creek Drive in Plano, a storefront location that formerly housed a synagogue and a Chinese music studio.

"There are no ghosts here, and we are just fine with that," Jamey said.

3

The Lonely Widow

If you want to hear some of the best stories of hauntings in downtown Plano, spend some time with Michael Hamilton. Now the co-owner of La Foofaraw, Michael has lived in the area since 1989—and has witnessed many unexplainable things in the downtown places where he worked and lived.

Twenty-three years ago, Michael and his family moved into the Lang House, as it happens, on Halloween weekend. As Michael arrived to deliver the family's last load of household items, the kids ran up to his car, looking like they'd seen a ghost. They'd been playing on the front lawn and insisted they'd heard someone beating on the windows inside the house, as if they didn't want to leave. Michael dismissed the kids' story, assuming it was a product of their runaway Halloween imaginations.

The following weekend, family members posed on the front lawn for a holiday Christmas card portrait. The photographer took many different photos, at several different angles. This was before digital cameras were common, so the family sent the film to be developed.

When the photos came back, weirdly, the house appeared to be on fire.

"Every window seemed to have flames and smoke coming out of it," Michael said. He could find no explanation. There was no sun in the windows, no reflections that might create this illusion.

It was the first of many odd occurrences in the house.

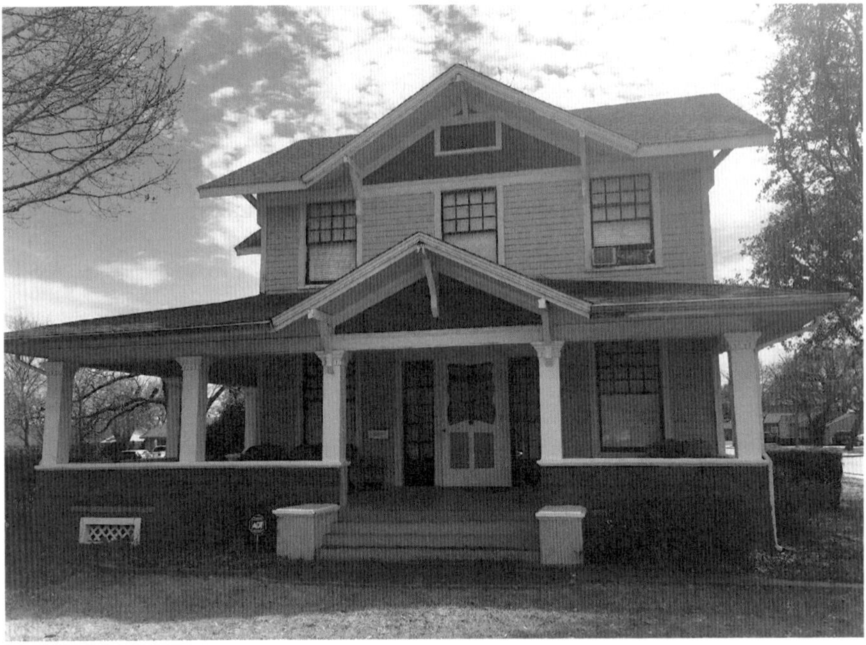

The Lang House. *Photo by the author.*

Unexplained Happenings

During the next three years, the Hamiltons lived contentedly in the Lang House. It was a happy, busy place. Children played in the yard. They landscaped and took good care of the house. The family loved to entertain. Sometimes as many as seventy-five people would turn up for dinner.

Then, Michael's family made the decision to purchase another house across the street, but they planned to remain in Lang House for another year while remodeling their new home.

"And that's when things started to go south," Michael said. "When we made that decision to buy the other home, weird stuff started to happen."

Bursts of mist suddenly appeared in rooms and then dissolved. Unexplained footsteps would startle family members as they sat downstairs in the living room. Sometimes the family's dog, Sunshine, sat at the foot of the stairs, looking up and down, as if watching someone or something coming down the staircase. The family would wake up in the morning and discover cupboards around the kitchen were open, even though they'd been closed the night before.

"This happened every morning for almost a year," Michael said. "The cupboards were very high—you'd need a ladder to access them—so it wasn't a matter of someone just forgetting to close them."

This presence, while mysterious, never felt malevolent. Michael Hamilton's theory is that the house's earlier occupant, a widow named Ms. Lang, simply didn't want the family to leave. While the Hamiltons lived there, the house was full of life.

"I think she truly felt like that house was alive again while we were there," Michael said. "I think these were signs that Ms. Lang was sending good vibes and making her presence known. I think she was pleased that her house was being well loved."

More Hauntings

At La Foofaraw, a boutique and gift shop on Fifteenth Street, neither Michael nor any of his colleagues have sensed any paranormal presences, even though it's an old building. (On rainy days, he and other employees do occasionally catch a whiff of wet soot, still present in the building's attic. "It's 150-year-old soot," Michael joked.)

But he's convinced that a nearby building is haunted, and that presence isn't as benign as the one his family encountered in the Lang House.

The building across the street, 1007 Fifteenth Street, is currently unoccupied but was home to Scrubs uniform shop until recently. Michael worked there in a boutique for several years in the early 1990s.

Often, he would work until midnight in the weeks leading up to the Christmas season. And sometimes weird things would happen.

"I would hear heavy thuds upstairs," he said. "Sometimes the elevator would go up and down for no reason, of its own volition." Other employees began hearing unexplained sounds. Some refused to work there alone. Female co-workers would wait for Michael to arrive in the morning before entering the place.

Then a new manager took over the boutique, and things really got strange.

"This woman was mean," Michael recalled. "She would stomp around the place, making the whole building shake. She would say things like, 'I'm closing this place down in five years.'" She seemed to have no interest in the business other than selling the shop soon and making life miserable for those who worked there in the meantime.

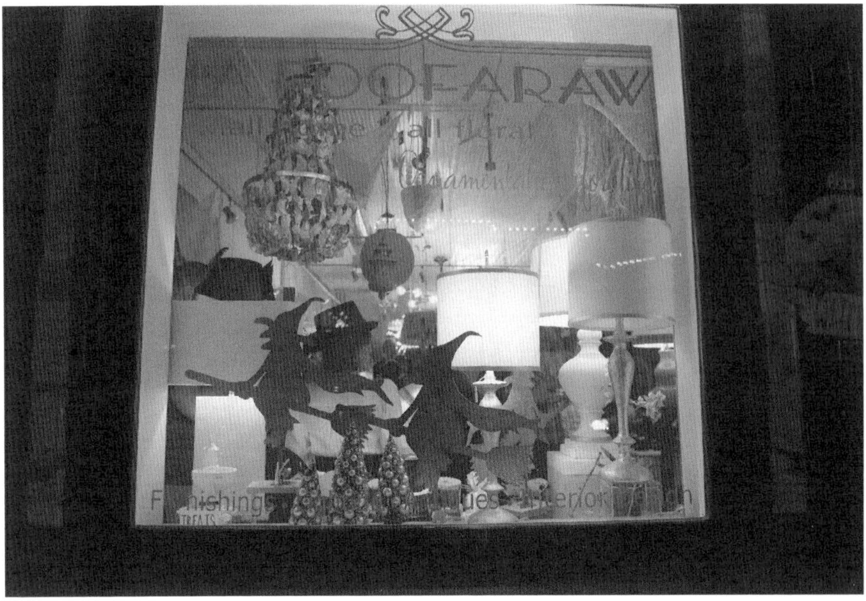

La Foofaraw in downtown Plano. *Photo by Debi Adams.*

One night, Michael was unwrapping a new set of Spode paper Santa Claus plates for a display in the store, when he and the manager started to argue.

Suddenly, it seemed as if the place was possessed.

"The paper plates literally stood up and spun around in the air. Things flew everywhere."

Michael has no explanation, supernatural or otherwise, for what happened in that building. But of this, he's certain: "That place has major mojo."

4
THE GIGGLING GHOST

At one time, the halls of the Cox Building were filled with children. Some say the spirit of one of those kids still roams the halls.

The two-story, Prairie Beaux Arts–style brick Cox Building was built in 1923. Until 1950, Cox was home to the entire Plano Independent School District—all children from kindergarten through twelfth grade. Now it's used for training rooms and offices, but there's also a small museum located in the building. It's a historic classroom with desks, a blackboard and other vintage school items. Until it closed in 2017, Theatre Britain performed on the small stage in the Cox Building's basement.

Veteran crew members of Theatre Britain believe the building is haunted.

One sound engineer refused to work alone in the building after an unnerving experience. Every time he put on his headset, he would hear sounds of a child giggling, completely unexplained.

It's just one of many strange incidents that he and other theater staffers attributed to a ghost they nicknamed "Peanut Butter Girl."

Peanut Butter Girl first revealed herself one night when a cast member left a jar of peanut butter in the break room. As it was every night, the theater space was locked when the crew left at night. Only two people had keys to the space. The next morning, the jar was open and smeared fingerprints of peanut butter were found all over the area.

Another time, the stage manager left all of the company's equipment plugged in after rehearsal, and the next day, it was all unplugged. No one in the crew would've considered unplugging the equipment, because some

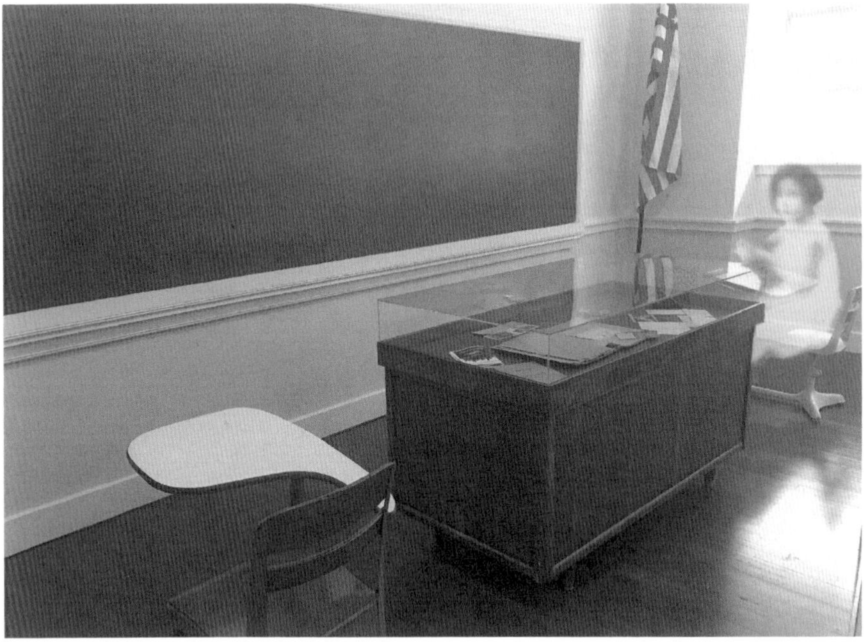

Is the Cox Building's Historic Classroom haunted by a giggling ghost? *Photoshop image by Brad Jones.*

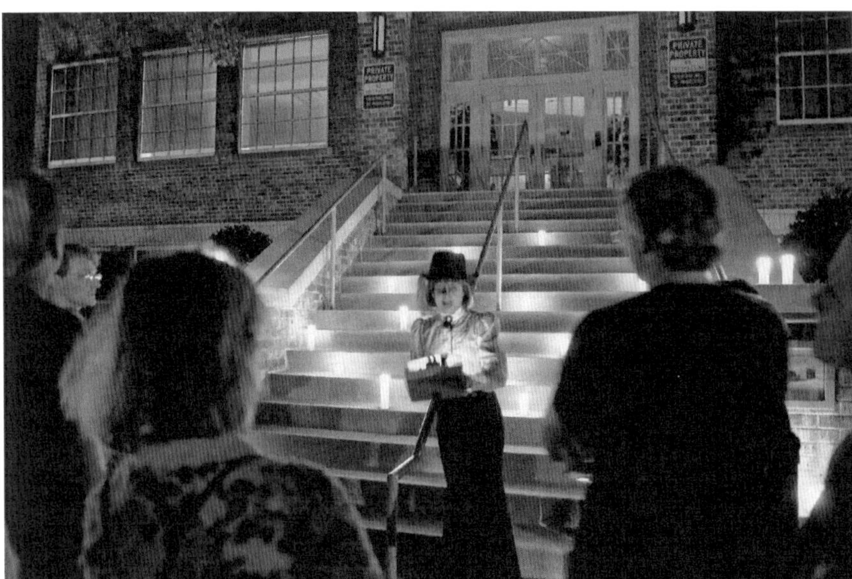

The Apparition Expedition ghost tour stopped outside the Cox Building, October 2017. *Photo by Debi Adams.*

is programmed specifically for each show, and by unplugging, they'd risk losing the programmed information. Again, the space was locked, and no one had come through.

The stage crew's theory: "Peanut Butter Girl" is the ghost of a schoolgirl who once roamed the halls and now resides in the historic classroom. She seems like a friendly sprite—just a little girl with a slightly ornery streak, who loves a good prank. And peanut butter.

5

The Phantom Pianist

Faint, phantom strains of piano music. Sounds of children playing. A wraith in Edwardian dress wandering the halls. These are just a few of the strange happenings reported by current and former residents of the Carpenter House, a beautiful Queen Anne Victorian mansion in the downtown area.

Because they were built with wood, many of Plano's historic buildings were destroyed in fires in the late nineteenth century. However, the Carpenter House was spared. It's a beautiful example of an upscale turn-of-the-century home.

The house was built in 1898 for Colonel Henry C. Overaker and his new bride. However, it's called the Carpenter House after its second owner, Gipson Edgar Carpenter.

If you've seen the house, you're probably not surprised that it's haunted.

"You can almost hear the walls talk about what must have gone on here," a former owner, Pat Black, told the *Plano Star-Courier* in 2013.

And maybe those walls do talk. Or play music. Past owners reported hearing piano music—unexplained—while in the house. Carpenter's wife played the piano, which was likely situated in the front parlor's bay window. She enjoyed playing in the afternoons, with the windows open, and reportedly, passersby would stop and listen. There are also rumors of unexplained sounds of children playing and footsteps on the stairs.

Leesie Pool and her husband now own the home. If anybody can coexist happily with the spirits of Carpenter House, it's Leesie. She identifies as a witch and loves vintage clothing. Sometimes she wears corsets, tightening

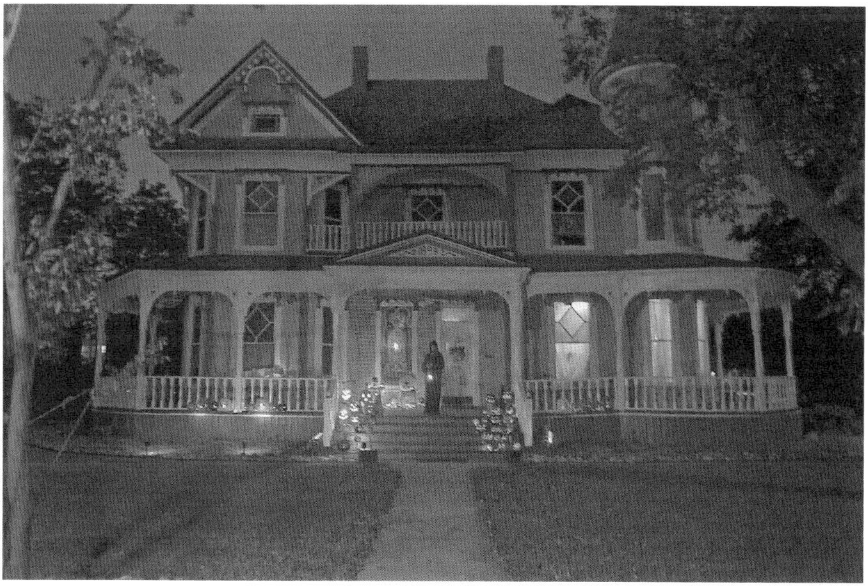

The Carpenter House. *Photo by Debi Adams.*

the stays to create the tiny waist befitting a Victorian lady. She has filled the lovely old home with goth mementos and vintage knickknacks.

Leesie once spotted an apparition—a woman in a long Edwardian gown, who appeared in the corner of her eye while she was upstairs—just for a moment.

Leesie wasn't frightened by the presence.

"I sense her presence in the house, but it's not malevolent," she said.

About the Carpenter House

The house was originally commissioned by Overaker, a prominent Plano resident whose business interests included lumber, agriculture, banking, a general store and postal service. At the time, it was set in the middle of a former cotton field, part of the colonel's many land holdings.

It took three years to complete the house, which Overaker had built with entertaining in mind. Many of its original fixtures remain to this day, including an indoor well and hand-carved panels that accent the corners of the home's door frames.

"He really spared no expense in the construction of the house," said Pat Black.

After Overaker died in 1919, the property was purchased by Gipson Carpenter, a prominent teacher, lawyer and farmer who served as a city attorney, council member and mayor. Carpenter Middle School is named for Gipson's father, Robert Washington Carpenter. The house stayed in the Carpenter family until the 1950s.

In 1976, Plano mayor James Edwards purchased the home. The house became a business in 1992, when it became a wedding venue. The Black family purchased the home in 2000 and owned it until 2013. During that time, they estimated about four thousand guests came through the Carpenter House.

By 2012, the Carpenter House's run as a wedding venue ended. Neighbors complained about noise and parking, and the city learned that the property's zoning didn't allow this type of operation. Plano City Council declined to allow the owners to continue to host weddings and other events.

Now a private home, the Carpenter House is here to stay. It was designated as a Plano Heritage site in the 1980s and is one of only two examples of homes of its type in Plano. The other, the Roller House, is around the corner on Fifteenth Street.

6

The Spooky Spinster

Several years ago, Debbie Holman invited a friend, a fairly prominent psychic in Dallas, to visit her home on Eighteenth Street in Plano. It was simply a social visit; Debbie hadn't asked her to check out the house for paranormal activity. But as she walked through, the psychic stopped abruptly.

"What is it?" Debbie asked.

The psychic had seen a vision, just for a moment.

"I saw a woman standing in the kitchen by the sink," she said. "She was wearing an Edwardian dress and with her hair up."

So, who was this specter?

A Single Lady

Debbie and her husband, Tony, live and operate a small business, Holman Pottery, in the Folk Victorian–style home built in 1890 by Fred Schimelpfenig, one of Plano's founding fathers and a prominent businessman.

Debbie did some research and believes her psychic friend had a vision of Lydia Mary—the spinster who bought the home from her father and lived in the Holmans' house, alone, for about fifteen years.

Originally, Fred built the home as a rental property, but in 1905, he sold it to Lydia Mary for $2,000, just a few days after her twenty-first birthday.

This was an unusual situation. At the time, few women owned property; most women married and relied on their husbands financially. So why did Fred sell such a large (3,200-square-foot) home to Lydia Mary, a single woman?

The psychic knew nothing about the house's history and had never seen the photo before, but as you can see, Lydia Mary wore Edwardian clothing, with her hair up. When Debbie showed her the photo, she said, "Yes, that's her."

Lydia Mary lived in the house until just a few years before her death, at age forty, in 1924. The cause of death listed on her death certificate was officially "Chronic Anemia," but some records say she had a "skin affliction." Descendants of the family recalled stories of trips to see doctors in other cities, to no avail. She never married.

So why did she own her own home, rather than living with her parents, as would've been the custom at the time? Possibly, Fred Schimelpfenig suspected, for whatever reason, that his daughter was not likely to

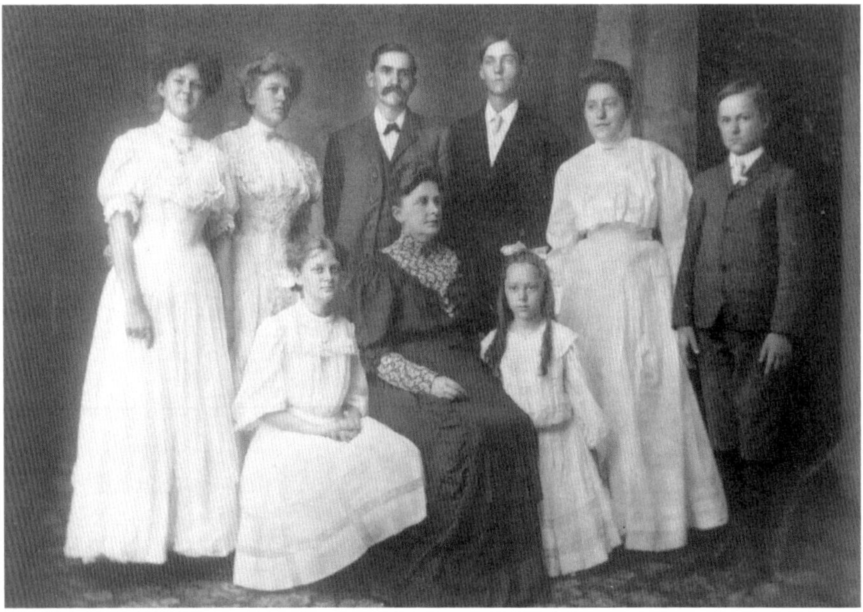

The Schimelpfenig family. Although the records are not clear, it's believed that Lydia Mary is second from the left, top row, in the photo. *Courtesy of the Genealogy Center, Plano Public Library.*

ever marry. Unmarried women were financially vulnerable at that time. Perhaps Fred put the home in Lydia Mary's name as a way of ensuring she'd be provided for. Maybe she was sickly or had some kind of disability.

Or maybe she was just odd or eccentric, which in those days, likely would have prevented her from marrying.

At any rate, if it's Lydia Mary who is haunting this house, Debbie's sense is that hers is a calm and friendly spirit.

"I've felt a presence," Debbie says. "It's a peaceful presence."

Debbie believes Lydia Mary was content while she lived in the house. She had her own place but wouldn't have been lonely with her family next door.

The psychic had a second vision in the home: in the pottery studio, where Debbie's husband works during the day, she pictured a dining room table, beautifully appointed, ready to serve a meal.

Neither vision frightens Debbie; she feels only positive vibes from the spirits who reside in her home. Plano was a prosperous town during Lydia Mary's time (and most of its history, for that matter) and fairly peaceful. So maybe that's why many of the ghosts who haunt downtown buildings seem to be, for the most part, friendly spirits.

But the Holmans also learned that the house has a sad history as well.

Two Wives, Gone Too Soon

Many families cared for their dead at home and had funerals in the front parlor, which was usually the best room in the house for that very reason. When you visit old houses in Plano, you can imagine how eerie it might have been, sitting at home alone at night, with your departed loved one in the next room.

And you can imagine how difficult it must have been for Roy Robbins, the man who lived in the house between 1922 and about 1934. Just three years after he moved into the house, his wife, Bertie, passed away. Roy remarried and, in 1931, had a son named Bill. Then Roy's second wife passed away from cancer just a few years later.

After the Holmans moved in, they had a visitor: an elderly man named Bill Robbins.

"That's not that unusual when you live in an old home," Debbie noted. "People stop by and say, 'Oh, I used to live in this house.'"

Even though he was only three years old at the time, Bill had a very vivid memory of his mother's body laid out in a coffin right there in the front parlor.

Not surprisingly, Bill said his father couldn't stand to live in the house any longer. Father and son moved out not very long after the funeral.

About the Schimelpfenigs

The Schimelpfenig name is familiar to anyone who lives in Plano. There's a library as well as a school in Plano that bear the names of Lydia Mary's parents, and descendants of the Schimelpfenigs are still living in Plano.

Schimelpfenig Middle School opened in the fall of 1980 with 410 sixth and seventh grade students and is named after Fred Schimelpfenig. Earlier that same year, Schimelpfenig Library opened, named after Lydia Mary's mother, Louise Ernestine Rammers Schimelpfenig.

Frederick "Fred" Schimelpfenig (1852–1942) served as Plano's mayor from 1902 to 1908. He was the owner/operator of a lumber company as well as a dry goods store. He began the first Plano Music Conservatory and devoted sixty-five years to serving on the Board of Stewards at the Plano Methodist Church, now the First United Methodist Church of Plano.

Louise Ernestine Rammers (1857–1907) was born in Louisville, Kentucky. She married Fred Schimelpfenig in 1876, and they moved to Plano two years later. Mrs. Schimelpfenig was active in church work and the temperance movement; she helped drive liquor and saloons out of Plano. She lent books to girls in the community, providing the city's earliest library service in her home.

Mrs. Schimelpfenig played an important role in the early days of First United Methodist Church of Plano. She hosted the first meeting of the Woman's Parsonage and Home Missionary Society in her home in 1880. The name changed many times over the years, but the organization remains active today under the name of United Methodist Women (UMW). The L.E.R. Schimelpfenig Circle of the UMW continues to meet, every second Monday of the month, in members' homes.

In 1884, Mrs. Schimelpfenig organized the Juvenile Missionary and Aid Society for Girls with twenty charter members. The society met one Sunday afternoon each month for fourteen years in the Schimelpfenig home. Mrs. Schimelpfenig also organized and taught the Young Ladies' Sunday School Class between the years 1882 and 1907. She kept a record of the class Bible readings, prayer life and all of its activities, and in 1908, after she passed away, the class was named in her honor. When you consider all of her civic accomplishments, on top of raising seven children (an eighth child died in infancy), it's hard to believe that Mrs. Schimelpfenig died at the relatively young age of fifty.

Mrs. Schimelpfenig also served as church organist for a time, as did her daughter, Irene. Irene Schimelpfenig Schell (Mrs. A.R. Schell Jr.) was an active member of the church until her death in 1983.

Members of the Schimelpfenig family, including Lydia Mary, are buried in old Plano Mutual Cemetery at Eighteenth Street and Jupiter, as is Roy Robbins's first wife, Bertie Robbins.

7
The Haughty Hostess

Keri Fleming will tell you that the ArtCentre of Plano is *not* haunted. However, she might allow that its current location, formerly known as the Saigling House, is paranormally active.

"We rent the space to brides and others hosting special events, so we never say it's haunted," she said. "But we have had many weird, unexplained things happen here."

It's not horror film fodder—no shrieking apparitions or howling poltergeists—just an accumulation of strange little occurrences that don't quite add up.

One staff member might leave all the shades up at the end of the day, and when the first person arrives the next morning, the shades are found back down again. Or Keri might lock the door to the basement at the end of the day, only to find it unlocked when returning the next day.

"I'll ask everyone: 'Did you go into the basement?'" Keri said. "Nobody did."

One time, Keri and a couple of visitors got stuck in the elevator. An uncanny set of coincidences led to the mishap.

"It seemed like something was conspiring against us," Keri recalled.

> *I never use the elevator at night, but there was a person in a wheelchair with me. I always have my cellphone with me, but this time I left it outside of the elevator. The call button, which alerts the fire department, always worked, until we got stuck. Then it wouldn't work. But after we were able to get*

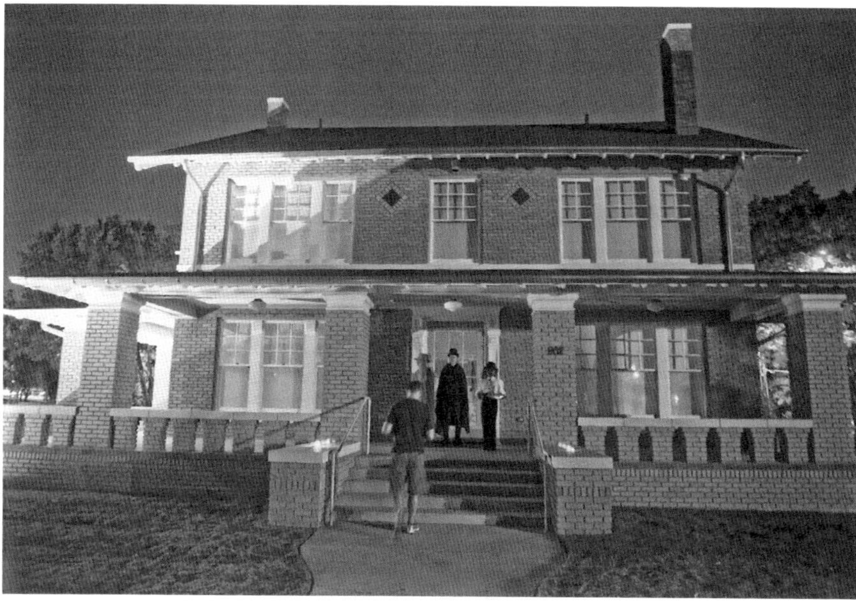

The exterior of ArtCentre of Plano, October 2017. *Photo by Debi Adams.*

> *out, the call button started working again and still does. We were never able to find the problem.*

Keri links the strange occurrences to Celestine Saigling, the home's original occupant. According to relatives, Celestine was a very proper woman. Maybe she doesn't appreciate all the "strangers" who come and go in her home now.

Charles and Celestine Saigling operated prosperous milling and lumbering businesses in Plano at the beginning of the twentieth century. After Charles passed away, Celeste built one of Plano's finest and most modern homes at the time in 1917. The Saigling house was one of the first brick buildings in town as well as one of the first to have a basement and central heating.

Celestine remained in the house until 1932 but didn't strike folks as a happy or contented resident.

At one time, her two granddaughters lived with her so that they could attend high school in what is now the Cox Building. (The girls' family farm, just a few miles away, was way too far for a daily commute by horse.) Stories passed down by the girls also confirmed her strict persona.

Rick Saigling, a descendant, said his father remembered Celestine as a "very stern" person. During Christmas dinner, the children were required

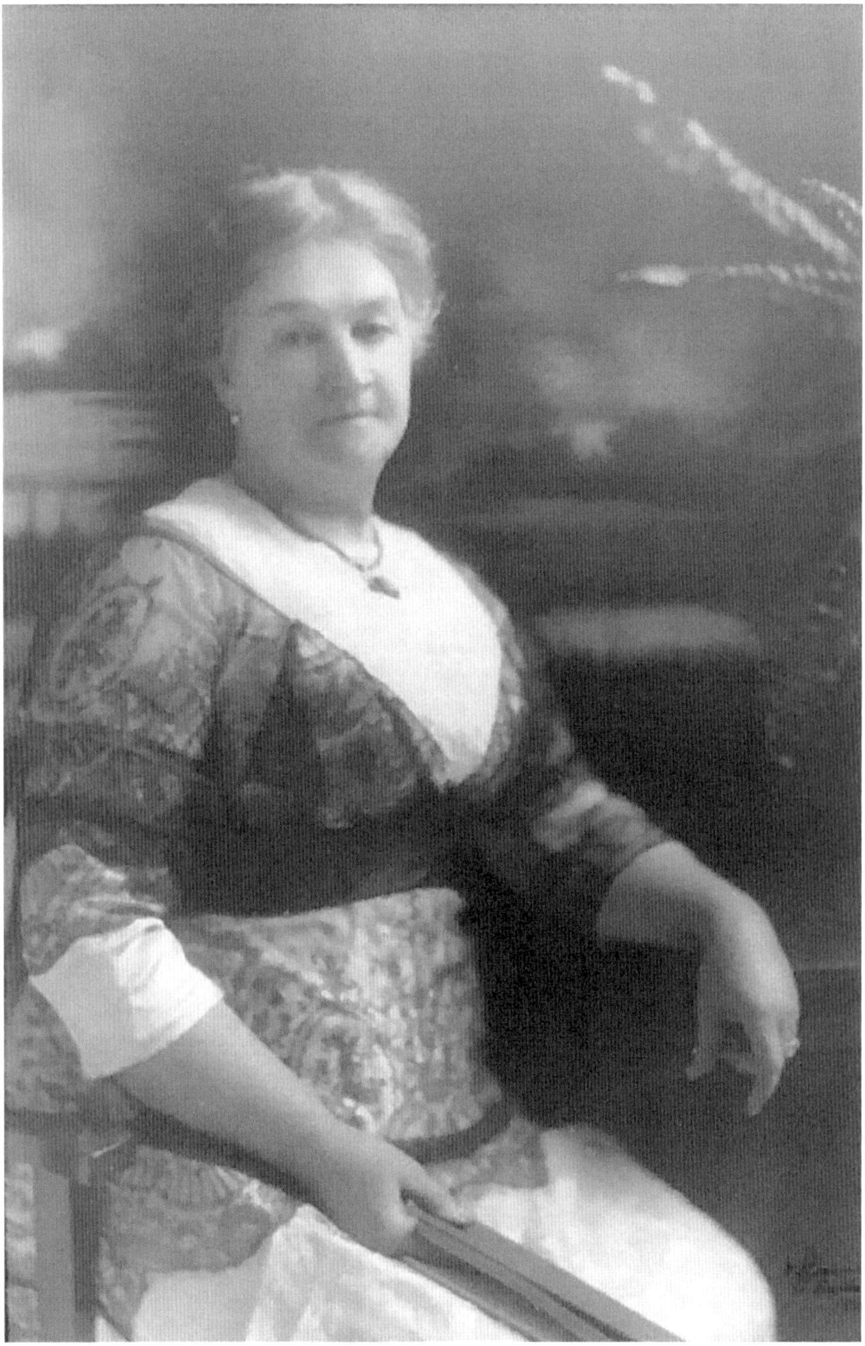

Celestine Saigling. *Photo by Steve Lavine.*

to wait in the hallway while the grownups ate. Only after the adults were finished were they allowed to eat.

"She apparently had very definite ideas about how children should stay in their place," Rick said.

Celestine may be unhappy that her home was turned into such a public place. Maybe she's miffed that unfamiliar people are constantly coming and going for weddings and parties and art gallery openings. Maybe she wants the home to herself, quiet and uninvaded by hoi polloi.

So, is it Celestine who's closing the shades, unlocking the doors or making mischief with the elevator?

That's what Keri believes. It's just a theory, but she thinks Celestine continues to maintain her position as the doyenne of this grand old home by playing little tricks that spook employees and occasionally unnerve the visitors, making the ArtCentre of Plano a little bit mysterious.

But remember, as Keri insists, it's not haunted.

8
HERITAGE FARM HAUNTINGS

Backpackerverse.com recently named Heritage Farmstead in Plano as one of "10 Haunted Day Trips in Texas That Will Make You Tremble with Fear."[5]

The scary spot at the Farmstead? The one-room schoolhouse.

Oddly, the schoolhouse is one of the few buildings on the Farmstead grounds that is not all that old. It's a replica of an 1895 schoolhouse in Ponder, Texas, and was built in recent years.

But then again, who are we to question the logic of the spirits?

According to the website, the house is haunted by "a really nasty ghost of a woman" who was a teacher in Plano and who doesn't like children—particularly girls. After one young family encountered her, they swore they'd never return to the Farmstead again. The blog reported that the apparition lunged at the family's seven-year-old daughter and scratched her face. Terrified, "the girl screamed and pointed upwards, where her parents saw the vicious face of an old-fashioned school mistress glaring down at them."

Independent schoolhouses like this one sprang up around the countryside in the late nineteenth century. They often doubled as community centers (for voting and political speeches), as cultural centers (for plays and musical events) and even as places of worship on Sundays.

Like most one-room schoolhouses of the time, the Farmstead's is equipped with wooden desks and chairs, a teacher's desk, a coal stove, a blackboard and a U.S. flag with forty-five stars. Teachers would instruct

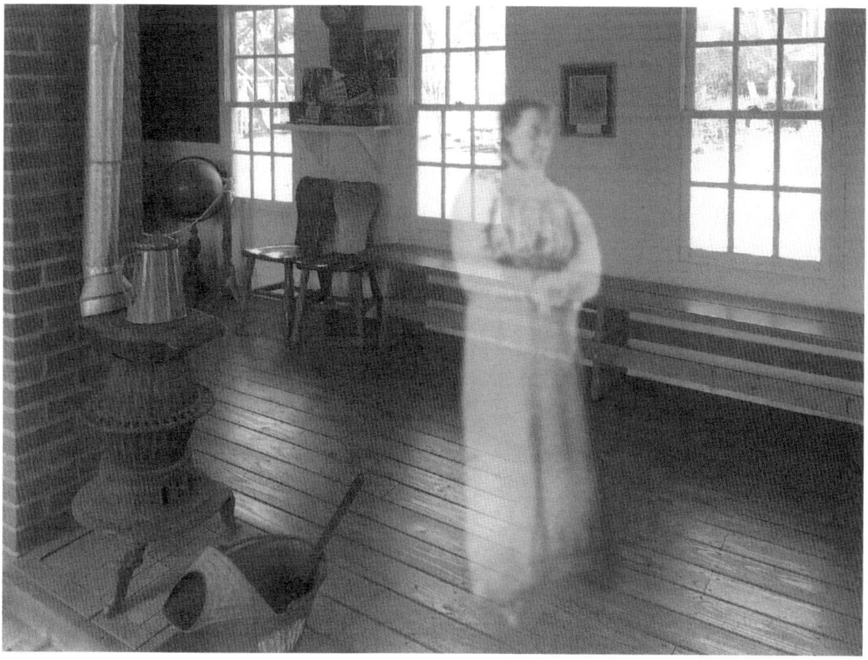

Inside the Heritage Farmstead Schoolhouse. *Photoshop image by Brad Jones.*

eight grades simultaneously, with the older students pitching in to help teach the young ones.

If you visit the schoolhouse, you'll see the one-room building furnished with vintage items: textbooks, lunchboxes and other paraphernalia. A potbelly stove, located in the center of the room, would've kept students warm on frosty winter days. And you'll also see, on display, a photo of a classroom of students with a rather daunting-looking teacher presiding over her young charges.

STRONG SPIRITS, STILL "ALIVE"

But ask the Farmstead's staff members, and they might tell you that the real haunted action takes place in the Farrell-Wilson home, the fourteen-room Victorian home built in 1891 that is the Farmstead's centerpiece.

"There's been some things that have happened here that can't be explained," as one staffer puts it.

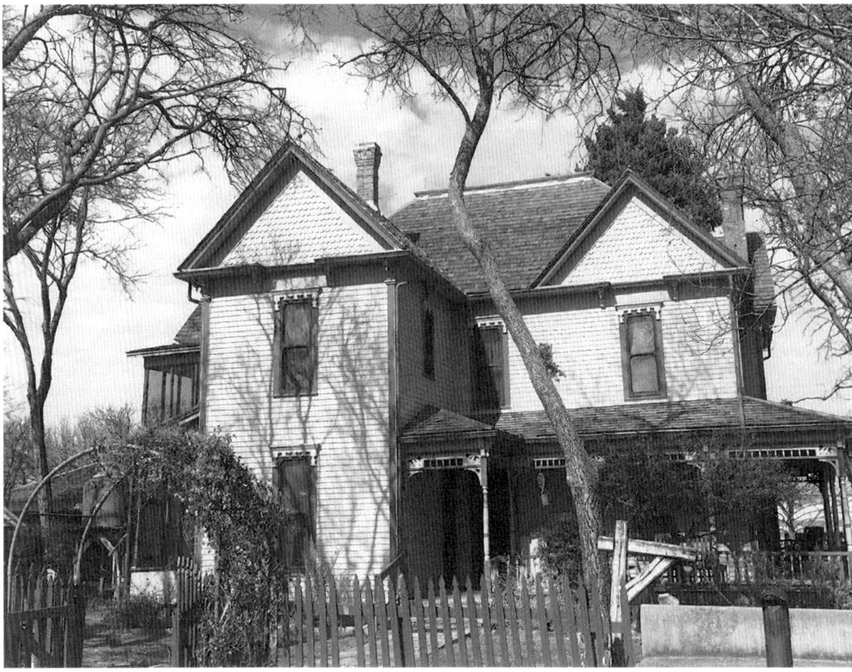

The Farrell-Wilson House. *Photo by the author.*

Mysterious odors have been reported. Several people have reported smelling cigar smoke, and others have detected the strong smell of roses at a particular spot in the dining room. Staff members have heard tapping on the desk in the formal parlor. When prompted, whoever it was responded with more taps. Some have heard the sound of doors opening and someone walking up the stairs, even though they had confirmed that no one else was in the house. These have all happened to several different people at different times of the day. Sometimes they were alone; sometimes other people were with them.

Former Farmstead staff member Hillary Kidd actually tried a little amateur ghost-hunting in the house; she brought her own paranormal investigation equipment to the museum late one night along with two other staffers.

Hillary attempted to communicate with the spirits. After entering the house's music room, she asked any spirits to identify themselves: "If someone is here in the room with us, please make your presence known."

A few seconds later, someone—or something—plucked the strings of a banjo displayed in the room. Three people were in the room and heard the sound, and the moment was audio recorded.

"Later, we tried to re-create it by moving around, stepping on floorboards, anything to make the vibration that would cause the banjo noise, but nothing worked," Hillary said.

Hillary also reported an eerie feeling of being watched or not alone in the house, at times when she was alone—or so she thought.

"I have never had the feeling of anything bad or oppressive," said Hillary. "It's the opposite; it's a feeling of joy. Almost like you're being watched because the spirits are happy that you're taking care of the property."

RENEGADE WOMEN

Some believe that hauntings are the spiritual residue of forceful personalities. Their spirits are so strong that, even though their bodies have passed to the next realm, their spirits somehow still permeate this one.

If that's true, then no doubt it's the colorful former residents of the Farrell-Wilson house who still maintain their presence there.

The house is named for its original owners, Hunter and Mary Alice Farrell, and its subsequent occupant, Ammie Wilson, who lived in the house until her death in 1972.

Ammie Wilson and her mother, Mary Alice Farrell, "were both fiercely independent, strong-willed, charismatic renegade women who forged a life beyond the standard female roles deemed appropriate by society," according to *Never a Good Girl: The Renegade Spirit of the Farrell-Wilson Family* by Hillary Kidd and Jessica Bell (2013, Donning Company Publishers.)

When her first husband neglected and abused her, Mary Alice sued for divorce in 1889, a step that very few women were bold enough to take at that time.

At the divorce trial, one of the witnesses who testified convincingly on her behalf was a man named Hunter Farrell. He claimed he'd observed Mary Alice's husband mistreating her. The divorce was granted, with Mary Alice receiving full custody of her daughter.

A week later, Mary Alice married Hunter Farrell. You can imagine the scandal.

Hunter Farrell was a highly regarded businessman and a farmer—as well as a ladies' man with a penchant for other men's wives. Just a few years before marrying Mary Alice, he'd been part of another scandal involving a married woman and a tragic death.

In 1887, Charles Henry found Hunter Farrell in the bedroom with his wife, Ellen Henry. He tried to shoot Hunter, but the gun misfired. He had shot his wife, Ellen, mortally wounding her. After he was released from jail on bond, Charles Henry tried to kill Hunter Farrell, who again escaped. A trial ensued and was covered in the papers in lurid detail. Charles Henry was acquitted.[6]

A few years after they were wed, Hunter and Mary Alice occupied the fourteen-room Victorian house that's now the anchor of the Heritage Farmstead. Farrell's business often required him to leave Mary Alice alone. Being a strong-willed woman who knew what she wanted, she had no trouble running the farm in Farrell's absence and making decisions. But when Farrell returned to his philandering ways, Mary Alice refused to play the long-suffering spouse. In 1928, after Hunter Farrell was named in two lawsuits claiming infidelity with married women, Mary Alice divorced him, too.

Being a twice-divorced woman in the 1920s was positively scandalous, but Mary Alice forged ahead with life undaunted.

Despite the couple's tensions, Mary Alice's daughter Ammie (pronounced AY-mee) grew up adoring her stepfather. Hunter Farrell taught her to gamble, and she remained an avid poker player for the rest of her life. She married Dr. Wood W. Lynch in 1901 and had a son, George Hunter Lynch, a few years later. That marriage ended in divorce in 1914, and three months later, Ammie married Dudley Moore Wilson. This second marriage was a happy one and continued for over fifty years, until his death in 1968.

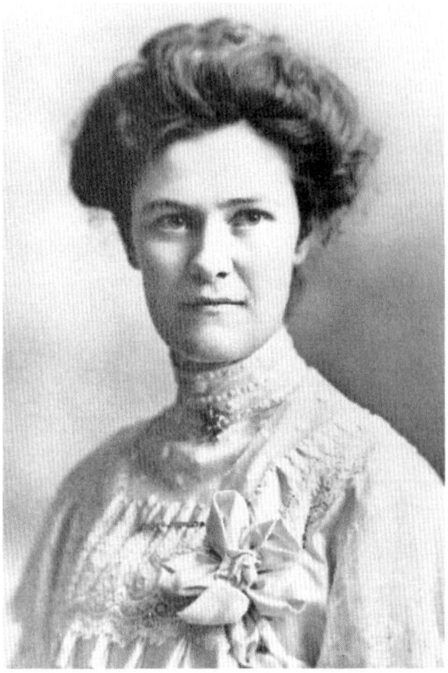

A young Ammie Wilson. *From the Frances Bates Wells Collection, courtesy of the Genealogy Center of the Plano Public Library.*

Ammie's son died in 1933, likely due to health problems related to alcoholism. Not long after, she threw herself into a new endeavor: raising sheep. By 1941, her life revolved around the sheep business. She was the only woman breeder in Texas, and her trophy room was filled with hundreds of ribbons won in competitions.

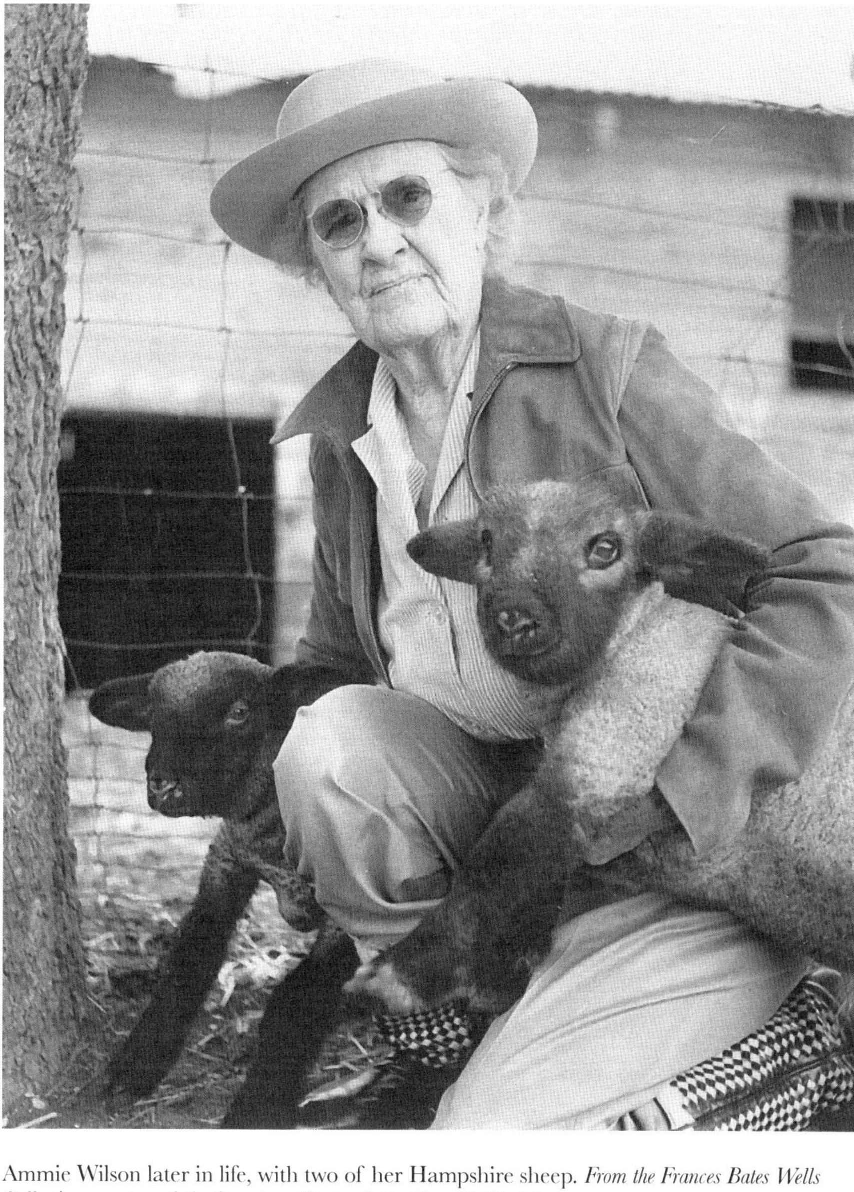

Ammie Wilson later in life, with two of her Hampshire sheep. *From the Frances Bates Wells Collection, courtesy of the Genealogy Center of the Plano Public Library.*

"I chose a man's work so that I could prove that I can do as good or better job than they do....I will get out of this business when I am too old to dream," she told a newspaper reporter in 1954. She smoked cigars and was known to employ a little salty language for emphasis now and then.

As a longtime friend wrote, Ammie was "a woman of courage and compassion, yet a very strong and demanding woman who could touch your life in a way you could not help from loving."

So it stands to reason: the strong spirits of Mary Alice Farrell and Ammie Wilson may still touch the lives of visitors at the Farmstead who are patient enough to wait and listen for their presence. What's not to love?

9

The Murdered Dentist

People come and go through the building at the corner of Fifteenth Street and Avenue K in downtown Plano. Some stop in to eat at ZaLat's, the pizza shop downstairs, or to work in offices upstairs occupied by a design firm and a photographer. And many of them have heard and seen some strange things.

At night, they've heard a woman's screams. Or unexplained footsteps. Sometimes, the footsteps sound like a woman in high heels.

Many years ago, a dentist maintained an office upstairs in the space now occupied by a photography studio, according to Connor Chaddick, who owns the building.

As the story goes, that dentist was murdered right there in his office. The dentist's wife showed up one day, found her husband in the embrace of his assistant and shot him.

The name of the dentist has been lost to history, and there's no date. Plano librarians have looked but never found any news reports of a murdered dentist in downtown Plano.

But Connor grew up hearing the story from family members. He thinks that, if there's any explanation for the sounds heard in the building, it's that they are echoes of the horrific event that family lore says took place there. He points to a rectangle marked in the floorboards upstairs, the very spot where the dentist's chair was once located and where the murder took place.

The Chaddick family legend says that the murderous wife was not tried, even though there was little doubt that she committed the murder. Maybe it was legal to shoot a cheating husband back in those days.

So those unexplained sounds of a woman screaming—were they the angry wife? Or the horrified assistant? We may never know.

WHEN COTTON WAS KING

In the nineteenth and early twentieth centuries, cotton was king in Plano. During the harvest season, streets were crowded, and farmers from all parts of the surrounding country came to trade and sell their cotton.

Originally, the building was one of five in the downtown area involved in the cotton trade. Connor Chaddick's grandfather W.H. Chaddick owned the 1896 building, which Connor inherited. Connor lives in Plano and manages the building.

On the K Avenue side, you can still see the remnants of pulleys that once lifted big bales of cotton into the storage loft. A skylight on the top floor allowed cotton buyers to inspect the bales.

The storefront downstairs was once home to Beaty Pharmacy, with a doctor's office in the back. Years ago, while re-doing the plumbing, the Chaddick family found apothecary bottles, embossed with these words: "Harry B. Beaty—Mechanic & Main." (Those are the former names of the streets where the building is located, Fifteenth Street and K Avenue.) Some of those bottles are now on display in the Interurban Museum.

But most Plano residents will recognize this building as the former location of the Queen of Hearts Magic Emporium. For more than twenty years, the shop was a favorite destination of kids searching for magic tricks, costumes and other unique treasures.

10

THE PARANORMAL PLAYMATE

Years ago, a family lived in the house at 910 Eighteenth Street, which is now home to a business, the Maid Brigade. The family began hearing strange sounds—footsteps and laughter, which sounded like a little boy playing.

The residents did some research and learned that a little boy had passed away at the age of about six in the Olney Davis House across the street. As the story goes, it took a long time for the undertaker to come and take the boy's body away for burial. The reasons for the delay are lost in time.

Was that the ghostly little guy that haunted the house across the street? Maybe, because it took so long to bury him, the little boy's spirit is restless. Or maybe, because the family living there had a little boy about the same age, he was looking for a playmate.

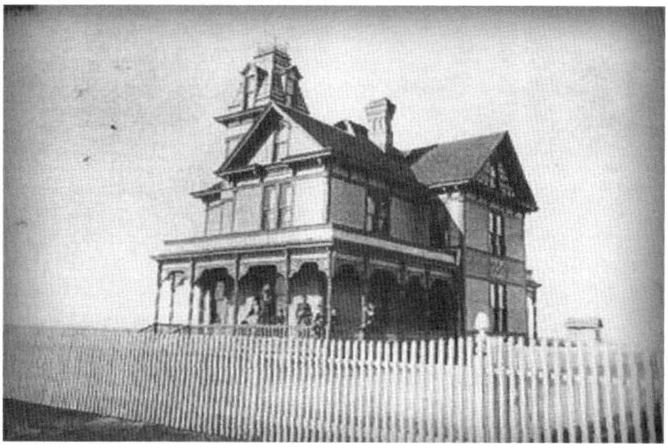

The Olney Davis House. *Courtesy of the Plano Public Library.*

Built around 1890, the Olney Davis House at 901 Eighteenth Street was originally the home of a Plano mayor and his family. Currently, the home is headquarters for City House Youth Resource Center and before that, the Art Centre of Plano.

Olney Davis served as Plano's mayor for two terms and was the first president of Plano School Board. Davis Elementary is named in his honor. Davis also was a prominent businessman with interests in lumber and cotton, a vice president of Plano National Bank and founder of Farmers and Merchants National Bank.

Olney and his wife, Effie, had nine children, two of whom died in infancy and a third, a little boy, named Raymond "Joe Bailey" Davis, who died in 1900 at the age of six or seven.

11
Ghosts around Town

Restless Roamings

Most of the folks who work at W&M Environmental Group, LLC, are engineers and scientists, so they're not inclined to flights of fancy. They're not the types who imagine ghosts or supernatural spirits lurking in every corner.

But some will tell you that the building they occupy at 906 Eighteenth Street feels a little haunted. It's an old house, built in 1916, with some sections added on later. Staff members have heard strange noises late at night—footsteps in the attic, creaking stairs, weird sounds in the crawlspace—or experienced a creepy sensation of not being alone, even when no other mortals were there.

About three years ago, the occupants learned of an eerie rumor that's linked to the old house.

"A middle-aged woman stopped by the house and said she had lived in the house," said Michael Whitehead, who owns the building. "She said that a young girl, about twelve or thirteen, had fallen down the stairs and died from her injuries years ago."

The woman added that she'd tripped on the stairs herself a few times, for no apparent reason. She believed the young girl's spirit was still present in the house. Maybe something about her death made her restless, and that's why she still roams the stairs and hallways.

"Maybe it was an accident, or maybe someone pushed her," Michael speculated. "Maybe she had some unresolved issue with a family member and that caused her to get angry and trip."

The woman also identified a portrait on the wall as that of the original owner.

That was a little unsettling, too.

"It reminded me of the portrait on the wall in an old TV series, *The Ghost and Mrs. Muir*," he said.

Michael hasn't experienced any strange sounds lately, partly because he no longer works with W&M. But he admits there's another explanation.

"To be honest, I've quit going there at night," Michael said.

The Phantom Bartender

When Toni Farris opened Yoga Tree at 1035 East Fifteenth Street about four years ago, she invited a psychic friend to help her move.

The friend told Toni that she sensed a "man from the old railway" living there and that the ghost had worked as a waiter back when the building was a saloon. According to the psychic, the ghost occupies the bathroom in the back of the building.

Toni's research confirmed that the building had once been a saloon, then a meeting hall for temperance crusaders, and ironically, it became a saloon again.

"I did not know that at the time," Toni said. It seemed a little eerie that the building's history matched the psychic's vision.

Toni hasn't heard or seen any evidence of the ghostly bartender herself, but customers do tell her the building has a "super nice vibe."

Is it the vibe of the bathroom-dwelling spirit? Or perhaps the karmic residue of the convivial moments shared in the saloon? Or maybe just good vibes acquired by the peaceful thoughts cultivated in the yoga classes?

Who knows? Maybe it's a combination of all of those.

The Jasper House

In the early 1960s, Kemper Smith was a kindergartner and lived with his family on Nineteenth Street. Every day, he and three friends walked to the private Happy Time Kindergarten near the railroad tracks and what is now the Cox Building.

On their way to and from school, the boys walked along Avenue H, passing an abandoned old dwelling that was later demolished, which Kemper believes was the Jasper House. No one lived in the home, and it was in pretty dilapidated shape.

Occasionally the boys spotted strange sights.

"I would swear to this day there was some kind of purple light in one room in that house," Kemper said. "We saw strange shadows, too. It was weird." Keep in mind that black lights weren't widely available at that time, so that's not a likely explanation for the violet glow.

The young boys soon became convinced that the old house was haunted. And of course, being boys, that led them to daring each other to go in.

At one point, one of the boys took up the dare, went up to a window and peeked inside. A moment later, he tore away from the house and back toward the road.

"He came back screaming and screaming," Kemper said. "He wouldn't say what he saw, but he definitely saw something."

12
The Zodiac Rider

If you're a skeptic, you might dismiss a vision reported by a paranormal investigator. But what if someone with firsthand knowledge later confirmed what the investigator saw?

That's what happened to staff members at the Interurban Railway Museum in historic downtown Plano.

The museum is housed in what was once the station for the Texas Electric Railway, which shuttled passengers and freight "every hour, every day" between Dallas and Sherman and points in between from 1908 until 1948. Parked next door is Car 360, one of the railcars that delivered mail, newspapers and passengers.

Several years ago, a paranormal researcher visited the museum and told the tour guide on duty that she sensed the presence of a spirit there. In her vision, she pictured a passenger, a woman, wearing a unique hat with zodiac symbols on it.

Museum officials didn't think much about the story until a few years later, when a longtime resident stopped in to visit. She had grown up in Plano and often rode the railway as a child in the 1940s.

One thing she remembered most vividly: a lady who always sat in the front seat behind the operator and who wore a pointed hat, colorfully festooned with stars, moons and asteroids. The lady was always dressed in black and sold small toys to children on the train for a nickel.

No one had told her about the paranormal researcher's vision.

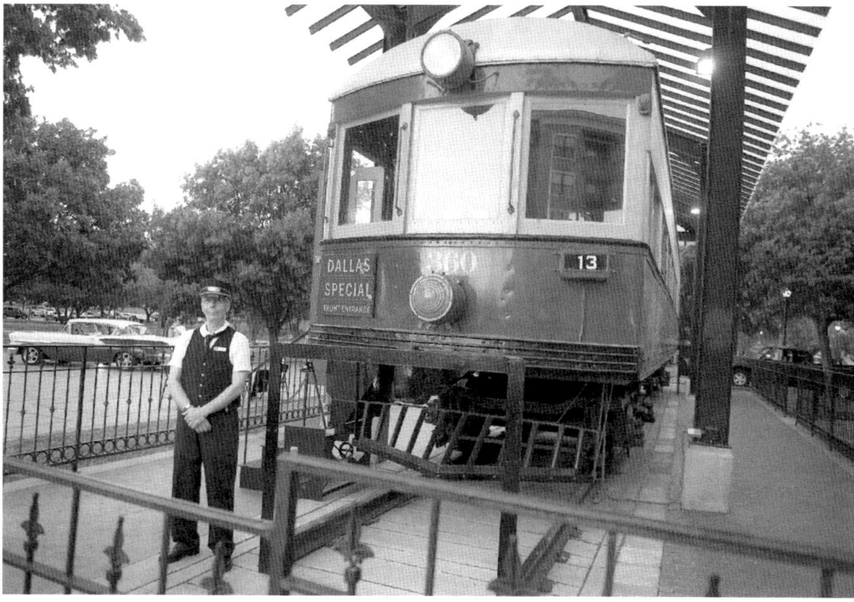

Car 360 and Motorman Jack. *Photo by Debi Adams.*

The visitor wrote about her memories later in the *Plano Star-Courier*, recalling how she chose items like celluloid glow-in-the-dark toys to take home for her box of treasures.

"That lady…was always on the interurban that picked us up in Plano," she said. "Now, as an adult, I wonder if there were several of these strangely dressed ladies with celestial goods for sale who made a living riding the rails and selling their wares to inquisitive little children."[7]

STILL RIDING THE RAILS?

Does the spirit of the Zodiac Rider—or Riders—still roam the railway museum? No one other than the paranormal researcher has reported any signs of her. But we can take some guesses about her story.

Possibly, she lived in a rural area. At the time, passengers who lived on farms along the railway could flag down the train, between stations, and purchase a ticket from the motorman. Maybe the Zodiac Rider was an older single woman—a widow, or a spinster, as she would've been called back then. Maybe she lived alone, maybe she was lonely and maybe she got a little strange.

Perhaps she whiled away the hours listening to a fortuneteller or astrologist on the radio. During the Depression, many local radio stations ran astrology programs that included strong appeals for donations to keep the show on the air.

ASTROLOGY IN THE 1930S

Baby boomers who grew up humming along to the "Age of Aquarius" may assume that the ancient tradition of astrology saw its first modern rebirth in the 1960s and 1970s. But astrology also enjoyed a spike of renewed interest in the 1930s, thanks largely to the radio and an astrologer named Evangeline Adams.

Adams, a descendant of John Quincy Adams, was a widely known socialite and radio personality whose circle of clients included famous names like J.P. Morgan and Enrico Caruso. Her CBS radio show, *Your Stars*, reached forty-four stations nationwide. She offered free horoscope readings to anyone who sent in four Forhan's toothpaste coupons; after only three months of broadcasting, she had reportedly received fifteen thousand letters. While fortunetelling was illegal at the time, Adams managed to duck prosecution by presenting her astrological material with the dignity of a society matron and with at least the patina of science.

At the same time, interest in astrology grew dramatically during the Great Depression, as desperate listeners sought guidance. Radio astrologers offered their insights while soliciting donations from listeners and peddling everything from toothpaste to nail polish and diet tea. And they were wildly popular. One astrologer, named Ethel Duncan, broadcasting in LA received eleven thousand letters a week; another, "Zomar," broadcasting out of a station in Birmingham, Alabama, received twenty thousand letters in his first four weeks on the air.

Local radio stations broadcast these commercial programs—which were essentially infomercials—during the Depression as a way to survive. Eventually, the Federal Communications Commission (FCC) judged the astrologers' broadcasts "indelicate and scandalous" and "intended to exploit and victimize the credulous." Wielding its power to grant or refuse license renewals, the FCC effectively censored these programs, and they eventually disappeared.[8]

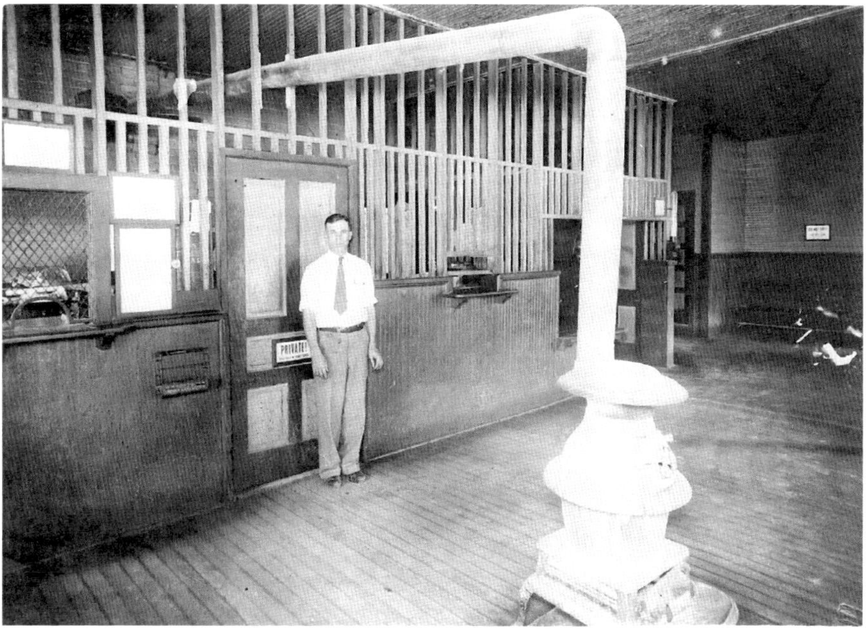

Interior of the interurban railway station. *Courtesy of the Genealogy Center of the Plano Public Library.*

We can only guess whether the Zodiac Rider picked up an interest in astrology by way of the radio or some other way or why she rode the rails and sold tokens and toys to the children. But she lives on in a treasured memory of one young passenger—now a mature lady—and perhaps haunts the Interurban Railway Museum and Car 360, if you have the paranormal ability to discern her presence.

13

THE UNCANNY COOK

Given that the Wooden Spoon is located in the Forman House, one of Plano's oldest homes, it's not surprising that owner Gwen Workman has encountered a few strange occurrences from time to time. Once, a psychic stopped in the shop and spotted a woman dressed in nineteenth-century garb.

Gwen has never heard or seen the otherworldly visitor, but she may have smelled evidence of her presence.

"I think she may like to cook, because every so often, we have cooking smells in this house that can't be explained," Gwen says. "Customers will come in and say, 'What are you cooking?' and I'm not."

There are a few restaurants in the area, but the odor doesn't smell like Mexican food or any of the cuisines offered nearby.

There's plenty of history to account for a few shadowy souls in Gwen's store, which specializes in all things Scandinavian. Joseph Forman built the Greek Revival–style home in 1867; his father, William Forman I, was the patriarch of one of Plano's founding families and served as the city's first postmaster.

Gwen is skeptical about ghosts, but she would love to tell you about a supernatural Scandinavian tradition that she remembers well: trolls.

"I grew up hearing, 'Don't go near the water; the trolls will get you' or 'Don't go near the woods, the trolls will get you,'" she said. "Basically, trolls serve as a scare tactic to make kids behave."

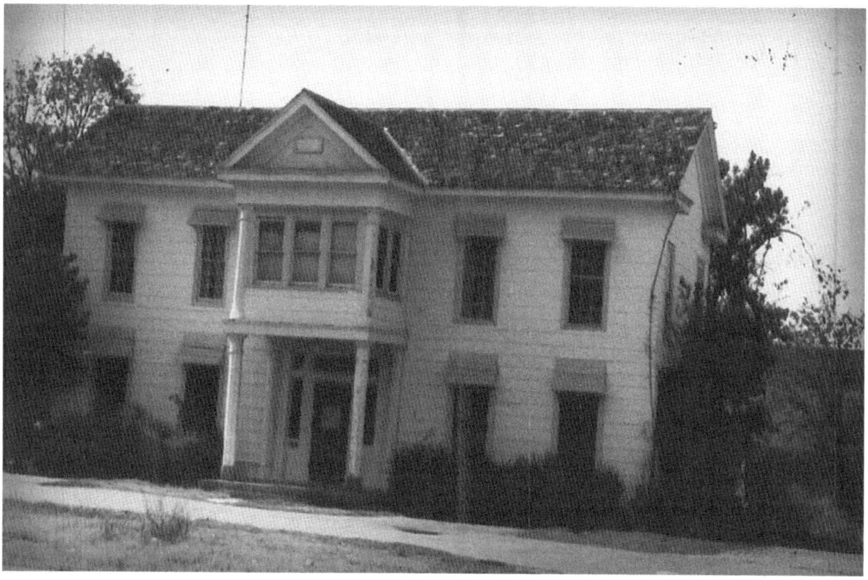

The Forman House. *Courtesy of the Plano Public Library.*

Gwen's customers have nicknamed the grassy median outside the shop the "Avenue of Trolls"—because, as the stories go, they live under the grass, protecting small insects and animals that live underground.

Many Scandinavian cultures have some tradition related to trolls, elves or other types of "hidden people." Surveys have shown that a majority of Icelanders either believe in the existence of elves or, at a minimum, won't say they don't exist. At times, construction projects in Iceland have been delayed or relocated to accommodate fears that the project was disturbing the elves.

Trolls are behind the name of Gwen's shop. In Scandinavian Christmas tradition, there's a character called the *nisse* or *tomten*. He looks a little like a garden gnome—a small person with a long beard and a red conical hat.

On Christmas Eve, families will set out a bowl of rice porridge in a wooden bowl and a spoon for the nisse/tomten. On Christmas morning, if the porridge is gone, that means the nisse/tomten will stay around for another year, acting as an invisible guardian spirit of the family and keeping them safe and prosperous.

To observe the tradition properly, it's important to leave a spoon carved out of wood, because, as the story goes, the hidden people detest metals.

Thus, the name of the shop: the Wooden Spoon.

PLANO'S NAME

Although its exact origin is a little unclear, some credit William Forman I as the man who named our fair city Plano.

In 1846, William and his family traveled from Kentucky to settle in Texas after purchasing the land in the Plano area. He became the area's first postmaster in 1852, with his home designated as the official post office of the community. Having a post office meant the settlement needed a name.

"From his home site on a hill east of the town, Forman looked out upon a flat prairieland," Rick Saigling wrote in a 2017 story in *Plano Magazine*. "To add a Spanish flair, he tacked on an 'o' to the word "plain" for his submission to the postal service."

Another theory credits the city's name to Dr. Henry Dye, Plano's first physician. According to this version, Dye submitted the name of Planno, which he mistakenly believed was the Spanish word for plain, when the first post office was established here. The extra *N* was eventually dropped.

Either way, the name of Plano was adopted with the blessing of the U.S. government.

The Formans prospered in Plano. In addition to farming, they built and operated two mills, a store, a distillery, a cooperage (to make barrels and kegs) and, eventually, a cotton gin.

In 1867, William's son, Joseph Forman, built the home that still stands at 1617 K Avenue, home to the Wooden Spoon. Forman Elementary School, off Shiloh Road in East Plano, is named for William. And at Plano Mutual Cemetery, you will find the grave of William Forman I, the man credited for giving Plano its name.

14
Who Ya Gonna Call?

A Visit to the Genealogy Center at Plano Public Library

Author's Note:
They're not exactly ghost hunters, but the staff at the Genealogy Center does hear from Plano residents looking for help with their ghosts. That's because the Genealogy Center fields all queries about local history that come to the Plano Public Library. We talked to genealogy librarian Cheryl Smith for a take on history and hauntings in Plano.

Q. Why do people call the Genealogy Library, and what help can you give?

A. People who are wondering, "Is my house haunted?" or "Is my apartment haunted?" want to know about the history of the place. They want to find out if something may have happened in that spot that could lead to paranormal activity, whether it's the land or the building itself.

Q. Have you found any history that might explain the hauntings?

A. We look at the history of the house or building and who lived there to see if anything might have happened to cause a haunting. We might look at who owned the place and see what we can find out about that person and his or her family. On several occasions, when the person reported a sense of being haunted, it did turn out that something a little spooky occurred in that place. Maybe somebody died there, for example.

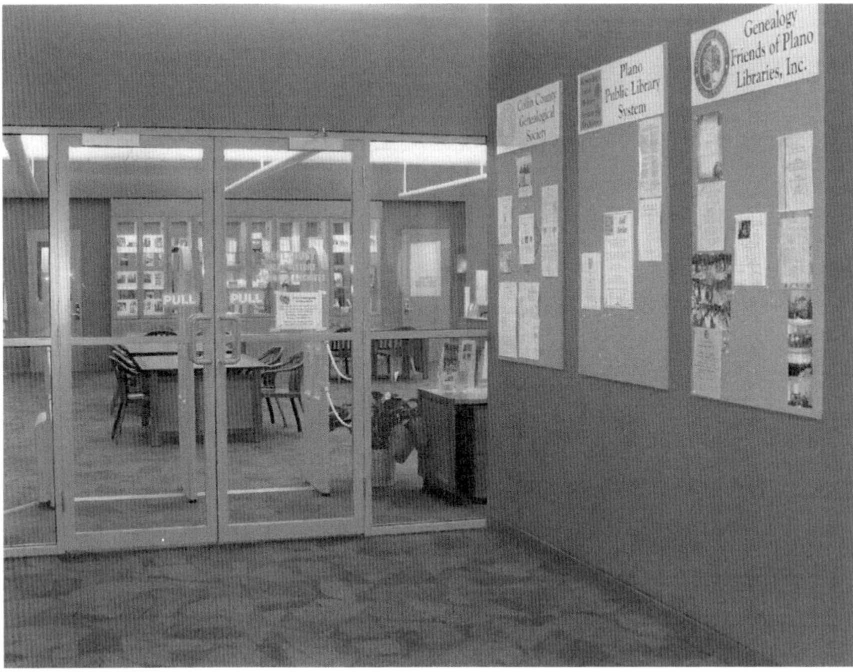

Exterior of the Genealogy Center. *Courtesy of the Plano Public Library.*

It's a little challenging with inquiries from residents who live in the apartment complexes in West Plano. That area was just farmland for so long that it's hard to know who owned the land or what could have happened. But if people are interested in the history of their home or their neighborhood, we're always ready to help. We'll do some looking and see what we can find out.

Q. Do you personally believe in ghosts?

A. It depends on what you mean. Are there visible, full-bodied apparitions that wander the earth? Probably not. I haven't seen any. But maybe there are spirits. There are things that happen that we can't always explain. So in that sense, yes. The idea isn't foreign to me. Growing up, my family's house was supposed to be haunted. Family members said they would hear crying in the cupola!

Q. What sorts of places are likely to be haunted?

A. Most people tend to believe that older houses or places are more likely to be haunted. But we have had people come in and say, "I think my apartment is haunted." Maybe something happened there. Who knows, maybe even a new building might be haunted.

It's possible that a terrible event could leave some kind of imprint in that area. Look at the Muncey incident. Could someone be walking around that area of Plano? Maybe. There was a school in Collin County that blew up in the early 1900s. Do some of those children still hang around? When something truly horrific happens in a place, or even just something that's very emotionally intense, it could leave an imprint.

Q. Tell us about some of the resources the genealogy library offers that citizens may not know about.

A. One of the most interesting things are the journals we have. They show what life was like in the early days of Plano. Typically, history puts so much focus on the big dates and the important people. But learning about what life was like for the average person at some point in history—that can be really fascinating.

At Haggard Library, we have bills from the 1840s and 1850s that show that a pair of denim jeans was $1.50. We have the diary of Lizzie Carpenter, a member of one of Plano's founding families. She wrote down everything she was doing. If you take the time to look through them, it really gives you a glimpse of life at that time.

Q. Ghost stories or no, why are you passionate about sharing Plano's history?

A. We have so many people who have moved here from other areas. It's important to learn the history. All of us on the staff here love researching the history of Plano. We love the stories. We learn something new nearly every day, and we want people to know about that.

III

Urban Legends

15
EDNA, THE BAD SEED?

In Bowman Cemetery, on Plano's east side, there's a row of headstones. They're the final resting places of five members of the Bowman family—and a source of sinister speculation.

Four of the tombstones are each carved with a single hand, holding a rose, pointing upward toward heaven. The fifth also has a hand, but that finger is pointing downward.

That's the tombstone of Edna Bowman, who died at the age of six, just a few days before Halloween in 1885. Over the years, that headstone has inspired a Halloween legend whispered among Plano's schoolchildren.

As the story goes, the finger on the tombstone pointed toward Edna's ultimate destination in the afterlife. Perhaps Edna was such an evil little girl, so mean, that her family knew she was doomed to Hades. Maybe, she was like Rhoda in the 1956 film *The Bad Seed*: the seemingly sweet, pigtailed little girl who's actually a heartless killer, whose mischief triggers fatal freak "accidents" for anyone who crosses her.

The five headstones stand silently along an alley, in view of passersby, creating a visible reminder that has likely helped keep this spine-tingling tale alive.

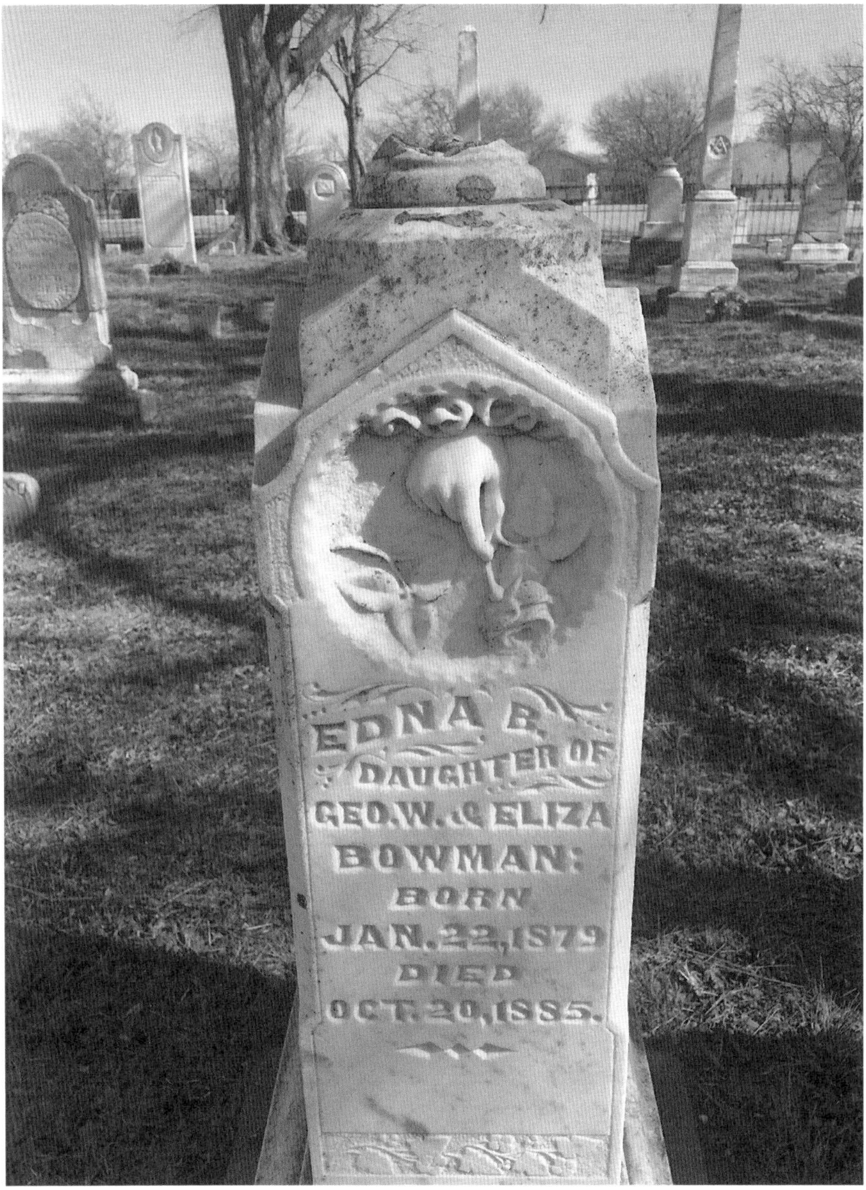

Above: Does Edna Bowman's tombstone point to her eternal destination? *Photo by the author.*

Opposite, top: Many late nineteenth-century tombstones featured an upward pointing hand. *Photo by the author.*

Opposite, bottom: The Bowman family's tombstones at Bowman Cemetery. *Photo by the author.*

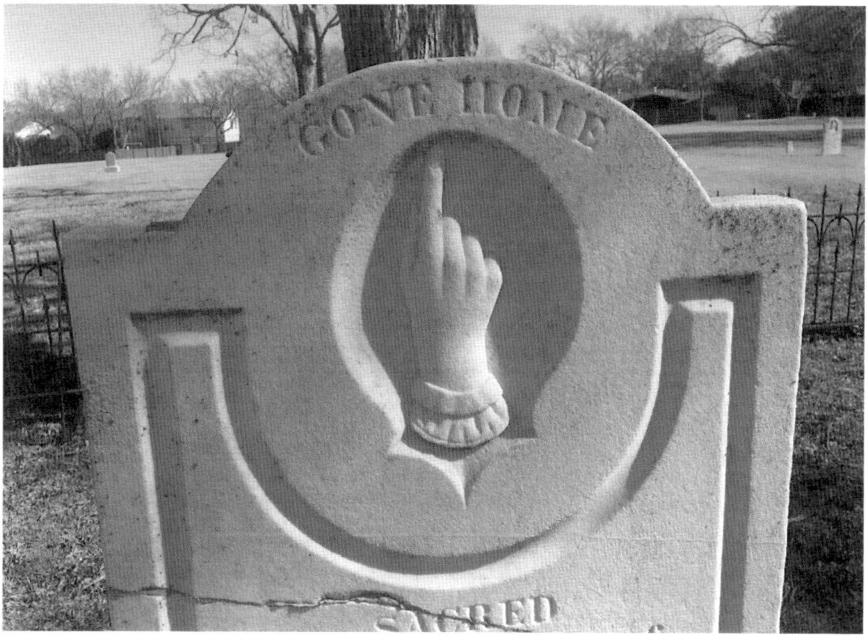
GONE HOME

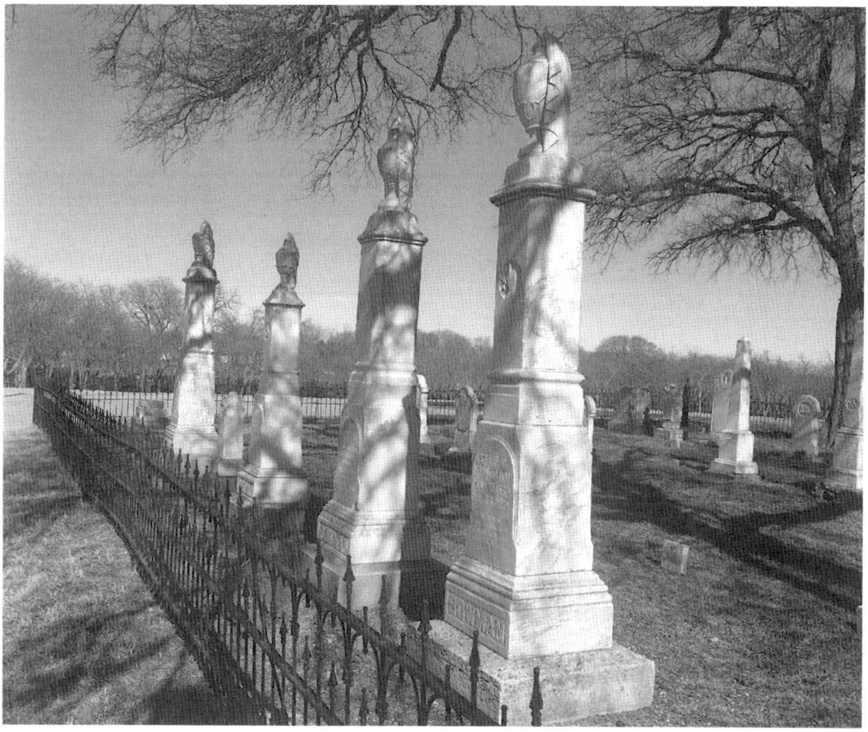

A Family, Resting Together

Also buried in that row are Edna's father, mother and brothers, George, Eliza, John and Joseph. When he passed away at age seventy-seven, George W. Bowman was the last marked burial in Bowman Cemetery. Sadly, all of George's family members preceded him in death: his wife, Eliza, died in 1890, as well as sons John and Joseph, who passed away at ages thirty-eight and twenty-two, respectively.

But the saddest of all, no doubt, was the passing of Edna, who was only six when she died in 1885. While the other headstones are beautiful, tall spires, Edna's is shorter, probably because she was so young.

Likely she died of one of the childhood diseases that took so many little ones at a young age in those days. It might have been a killer disease—like smallpox, cholera or typhus—or possibly a more minor ailment like strep throat that today could easily be treated with antibiotics. Many of Plano's pioneer cemeteries are full of gravestones marking the loss of little ones, a much more common occurrence at the time.

Every Halloween, Plano history advocates take pains to debunk the rumor that mars Edna's memory. The downward-pointing hand, which also holds a rose, didn't mean that Edna was headed to the bad place. In those days, a downward-pointing hand was a common symbol signifying a life taken too early or unexpectedly.

"Notice the clouds around the wrist of the hand," added Collin County history buff Joy Gough. "There is a common epitaph on children's graves at the time, that says, 'a flower that budded on earth to bloom in heaven.'" The finger's direction likely meant that God had taken the "budded flower" to heaven.

So, while the story of the "bad seed" makes for a great Halloween yarn, let's set the record straight for little Edna, clearly beloved and taken too soon. May she rest in peace.

About the Bowman Family

Edna was part of a prominent Plano family. George W. Bowman Middle School, at the intersection of Park and Jupiter, is named for her father. He and his brother, Jackson Harrison Bowman, came to Texas from Tennessee in 1857 with their parents.

A veteran of the Confederate army, George was an original organizer and investor of Plano's first bank, Plano National Bank. Bowman served as the bank's president for over thirty years until his death in 1921. He also held interests in several other business ventures and served for ten years on the Plano School Board.[9]

16
CLOWN THREAT

Clown Threat. Just putting these two words together seems a little laughable. But for a few weeks in 2016, clowns struck fear in the hearts of many Americans.

An epidemic of reports of encounters with scary clowns swept the country, and Plano was not immune. In fact, Plano saw the first confirmed case in North Texas.

In late September of that year, a resident, who asked not to be identified, told WFAA-TV that he had been confronted by a man in full clown regalia along Russell Creek in Plano. The victim was walking at around 8:45 p.m. when he heard a rustling of leaves and a pinging noise, possibly a baseball bat hitting a guard rail. That's when he met the creepy clown with a deep menacing voice and a bat in his right hand.

"The individual in the clown mask confronted our victim and said, 'Do you wanna play a game?'" Plano Police spokesman David Tilley told WFAA.[10]

That clown was apparently unaware that he'd chosen a six-foot, four-inch man with mixed martial arts experience as his victim. When the clown strode toward him, the man used one hand to shield the bat and the other to throw a punch. The victim believed he hit the clown in the face, as he saw blood dripping through the mask as the clown ran back into the woods.

Tilley told the TV reporter that, if it was a prank, it was neither funny nor safe.

"This can be a deadly game," Tilley said. "We're in Texas. People carry."

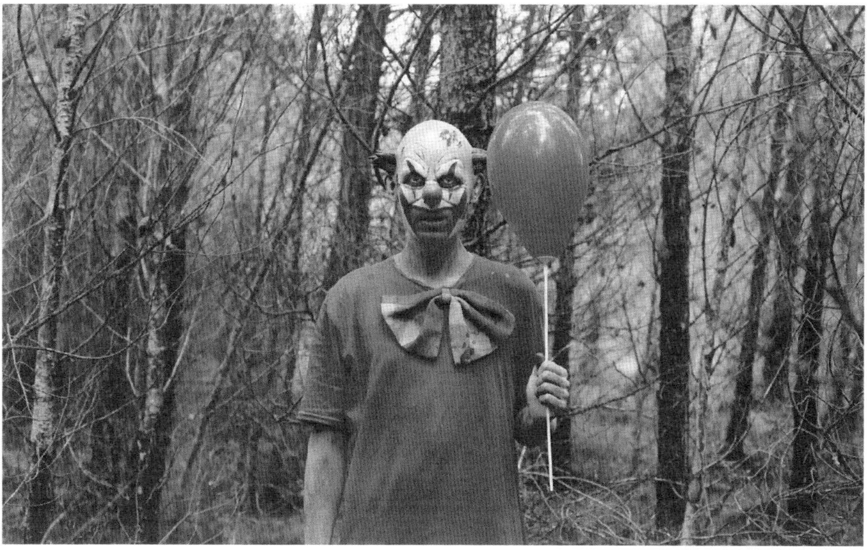

Clowns scared the wits out of Americans in 2016. Most threats weren't credible, but a Plano man did have a truly frightening clown encounter. *Shutterstock.*

NATIONWIDE SCARE

"Clown hysteria has taken the country by storm," warned an October 4, 2016 article in *Time* magazine. The frenzy began with unsubstantiated reports of clowns trying to lure children into the woods in South Carolina, North Carolina and Georgia. While searches of the areas had turned up nothing, reports of scary clown sightings soon followed in more than two dozen states from Alabama to Wisconsin.[11]

It's not clear whether the Plano clown was intent on truly doing harm or just a copycat playing a stunningly stupid prank. But given that the clown charged a grown man and was armed with a baseball bat, the Plano sighting may be one of the few truly threatening Clown Threats.

Most were hoaxes. Several so-called clown sightings involved young pranksters dressed as clowns or callers inventing clown stories. Many of the threats were made over social media, and most turned out like the incident in Des Moines, where two fourteen-year-old boys showed up at school wearing clown masks to scare friends.

After the incident, Des Moines Public Schools emphasized that "law enforcement, both locally and across the country has found no credibility in any of the threats being made as part of this hoax."[12] Similarly, police departments around the country, including the New York Police Department, issued statements to ease fears, noting that no Clown Threats had turned out to be credible.

Even horror novelist Stephen King tried to tamp down the terror, tweeting, "Hey, guys, time to cool the clown hysteria—most of 'em are good, cheer up the kiddies, make people laugh."

A few arrests did take place during the scare. In Alabama, at least seven people were charged with making terrorist threats connected to "clown-related activity," as Rainbow City police chief Jonathon Horton told the *Times-Picayune*.

The most horrific clown report came from a Reading, Pennsylvania neighborhood where a sixteen-year-old wearing a clown mask pushed up onto his head was fatally stabbed, but police blamed an argument, not a scary clown, for the incident.

Still, the wave of panic took on a life of its own. Hundreds of students at Pennsylvania State University swarmed surrounding campus streets to carry out a mass clown hunt. A Connecticut school district temporarily banned clown costumes and any "symbols of terror." And an armed clown hoax put a Massachusetts college on lockdown.

In New Haven, Connecticut, school officials banned clown costumes following several menacing clown-related social media posts, although the local police department spokesman admitted they had not seen anything "tangible."

"The fascination with clowns is really the fact that they're not real," Scott Bonn, a criminologist and professor of sociology at Drew University in New Jersey, told *Time*. "We don't know what's beneath that makeup. It could be anyone or anything. They're actually very frightening."

Perhaps hit hardest by the wave of fear was the professional clown community. Jordan Jones, who worked part-time portraying Snuggles the Clown in a haunted house, told *Time* magazine, "I fear for my life."

Jones went on to create a "Clown Lives Matter" movement on his Facebook page to draw attention to the plight of professional clowns.

"I'm not the enemy," he said.

The scary clown craze disappeared just as quickly as it arose. By the fall of 2017, clown sightings were long gone from the national radar.

Hollywood, however, still seemed intent on capitalizing on the fear, releasing a season of *American Horror Story* with a clown storyline and the much-hyped new film adaptation of Stephen King's *It*.

"The clowns never left," joked Kaitlyn Tiffany in a snarky post on the website the Verge. "They were just 'in development.'"

17

THE GOAT MAN

If you grew up in Plano in the 1950s, '60s and '70s, likely you heard this warning: Watch out for the Goat Man.

According to the legend, the Goat Man attended school in Plano in the 1940s and kept a herd of goats—until a group of teenagers went to the farm and decapitated the goats.

"It screwed him up bad enough where there were incidents in 1950 in which a couple of teenagers disappeared," former resident Kenny Smith told the *Plano Star-Courier*. "It even got to the point where there were kids that were drowning in the creek where Dublin Road crossed at the time." Blame fell on the Goat Man, allegedly the farmer turned maniacal murderer after his flock was killed—or perhaps, his ghost.

Goat Man supposedly lived in the woods along Rowlett Creek outside of Los Rios, under an old wooden bridge off Dublin Road, and that became a destination for thrill-seeking teens in Plano. High school athletes brought freshmen to the bridge at night for initiation purposes.

"If you had the guts to not believe the legend…then you could spend the night on the bridge," Smith said. "I never heard of anyone stupid enough to do that…if you spent the night, the ghost of the Goat Man would get you."

One Planoite remembers driving with friends to the bridge to listen for the Goat Man.

"We had to roll down the windows, unlock the doors, kill the engine and remove the keys from the ignition," she said. "The driver had to give the keys to someone in the backseat. Needless to say, we did not stay long. I swear we

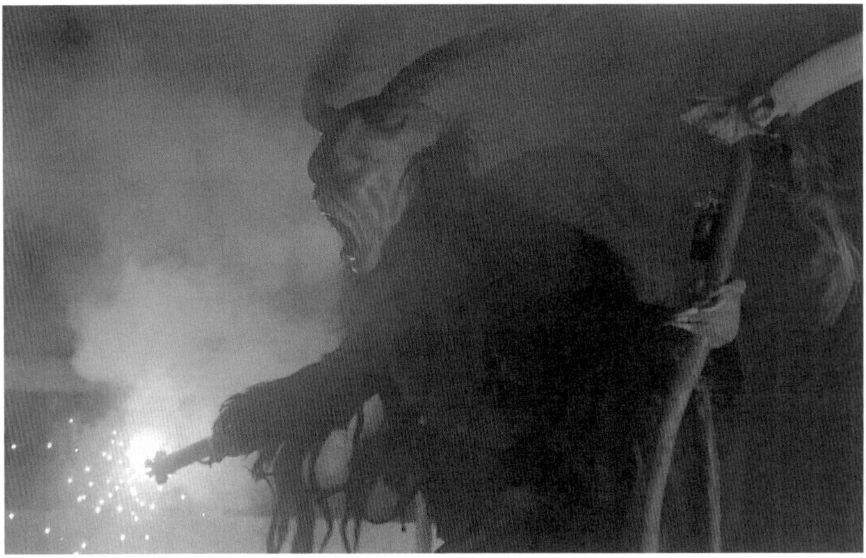

Several Plano residents swear they spotted the Goat Man off Dublin Road. *Shutterstock.*

could hear 'hoof' sounds on the rocks." Even though it was a long time ago, she added, the memory still spooks her.

Goat Man's Bridge was torn down in the 1980s, but the legend lived on, as the Goat Man was allegedly spotted in other parts of town.

Another longtime resident heard that if you trespassed at Los Rios Golf Club, then a half-man, half-goat would chase you and throw horse apples at you. He swore that a friend's tailgate was shot by the Goat Man.

Another reported seeing the Goat Man after sneaking out to Bob Woodruff Park one night with friends. "There was something out there," Barbie Oliver told the *Star-Courier*. "We swear to this day we saw him. If it wasn't him, someone was out there trying to scare us. We found a dead goat and got the hell out of there."

The Goat Man of Bob Woodruff Park had a different origin story than the farmer-turned-murderer Goat Man. In his story, his family had owned the land where the Goat Man roamed; after his parents died and the land was sold for development, he refused to leave.

"He roamed the woods at night, and if you were caught out there after dark, you would never be heard from again," Barbie said. There were rumors of missing people who'd been last seen in that area.

"All I know is I was a believer after that night," Barbie said. "Never would I even drive that way at night."

FUN WITH GOAT MAN

Not all stories about the Goat Man are strictly scary. "Looking for the Goat Man" became an excuse for nighttime gatherings that may have also involved drinking, smoking and making out in the areas Goat Man was rumored to roam.

The Goat Man also inspired a few pranks. "My brothers took me out there and scared the crap out of me," one resident commented on Facebook. "Leaving a nine-year-old on a dirt road with a bloodthirsty half-man half-goat on the loose."

Another resident played the Goat Man himself. "To this day, my friend still thinks he saw the Goat Man," he commented on Facebook. "I never had the heart to tell him it was me!"

No one has seen the Goat Man in recent years; as the large swaths of undeveloped land in Plano disappeared, so did the Goat Man. Some believe he's still out there—but development has pushed him to less inhabited areas far north of Plano.

Another longtime Planoite pleaded with people on Facebook to stop making jokes about the Goat Man.

"I've seen him gargle mossy creek water, and he will come after you," he warned. "I still remember the way he bleated…and those horrible red eyes."

Then, he quipped: "It's just funny.…I've wanted to make a 'Goat Man' movie for years."

STILL HAUNTED

There are two ways to be haunted: by a scary creature that makes your heart race or by way of a story that follows you the rest of your life. By the latter definition, no one has been more haunted by the Goat Man of Plano than Kemper Smith. Kemper grew up in Plano, graduated from Plano High School in 1974 and then enlisted in the navy.

"I told the story of the Goat Man to my navy shipmates," Kemper said. "They laughed, but the name stuck."

Kemper sports a long beard—one that brought a billy goat to mind for his shipmates. They ribbed him, saying that billy goats urinate in their own beards and wondering if Kemper might do the same.

Kemper was known as Goat Man during the entire six years he was active duty. And even now, more than thirty-five years later, he's still the Goat Man to the shipmates who still keep in touch. When one of them emails him, he signs off with a "Baaaaaa."

The Goat Men

It turns out that stories of murderous half-men, half-goats aren't unique to Plano. In Denton, the Goat Man is the most feared of all local ghosts. And the story is truly terrifying.

Travelers to the Old Alton Bridge have long reported frightening encounters. Built in 1884, it's a legendary spot for Texas ghost hunters.

The most familiar version of the story: an African American entrepreneur named Oscar Washburn and his family tended a goat herd near the bridge. Folks would travel out to his farm to buy its quality meat, milk, cheeses and hides. To help customers find their way, Oscar proudly hung a sign on the bridge, which read: "This way to the Goat Man."

Local Klansmen became infuriated, and one night in the late 1930s, they stormed the farmer's shack and dragged him to a noose on the bridge. But after they tightened the rope and flung Oscar over the side, he disappeared, leaving only an empty noose dangling over undisturbed waters.

The panicked Klansmen frantically searched the area before rushing to the shanty, setting it afire with the Goat Man's family shrieking inside, perhaps in a desperate attempt to lure Oscar out of hiding. The Goat Man was never seen again, as the story goes, but his vengeful spirit has haunted the Old Alton Bridge ever since.

Local legend says if you knock on the steel bridge three times at midnight or turn off your car lights and honk three times in summons, then the Goat Man may come for you. Reportedly, a visitation is always preceded by the stench of decaying flesh. Other reports tell of unholy glowing red eyes and glimpses of an eerie half-man, half-goat, stomping in the wooded shadows. The terrifying encounters and reported vanishings have been so frequent as to warrant numerous investigations by paranormal groups.

There is also another version of the story that predates the bridge itself. In the 1860s, some Copper Canyon cowboys lynched a Creole slave goat herder named Jack Kendall from a tree near where the bridge now stands. Somehow, the runaway slave's head separated from his body. As the story goes, the slavers then watched in horror as the headless body raised itself from the creek bed mud, animated by voodoo, and ripped off the head of a nearby goat to replace his own, still dangling in the noose.

MARYLAND'S GOAT MAN

Goat Men have also been spotted by multiple eyewitnesses in other states all over the country, including Maryland, Wisconsin and Kentucky.

The most famous Goat Man was first spotted in Prince Georges County, Maryland, where he reportedly has a lair under a rusty old bridge—Governor's Bridge. Get too close, and you might die, according to local lore.

This Goat Man story has a sci-fi twist. He was once a scientist who worked in the Beltsville Agricultural Research Center until an experiment involving goats went horribly wrong. The scientist was mutated, becoming goat-like himself.

Depending on who you ask, the Goat Man of Maryland roams the back roads of Beltsville, attacking cars with an axe, or he's an old hermit who lives in the woods, seen walking alone at night along Fletchertown Road.

University of Maryland folklorist Barry Pearson said the Goat Man legends began "long, long, long" ago and were reignited in 1971 when local residents blamed a dog's gruesome death on Goat Man. Pearson noted that "bored teenagers" keep the Goat Man legend alive by repeating the story and suggesting that the creature attacks couples frequenting the local lovers' lane

One thing's for sure: Maryland's Goat Man has earned a lot more publicity than Plano's Goat Man. He's appeared in two comic books (*Hellboy* and *X-Files*) and a reality show. And as recently as 2016, WBAL-TV viewers submitted photos of a mysterious beast that appeared at Montpelier Park in Laurel, Maryland. One described the animal as a "Sasquatch with horns."

Is the Goat Man a product of runaway imaginations? Bored teenagers? Or is it like Big Foot—what some insist is a real, unidentifiable beast that still roams Maryland's woods? You decide.

18

Stranger Things at Ranch 111

You won't find any newspaper reports, but in the 1970s and 1980s, everybody in Plano knew about Ranch 111—a wooded area where unspeakable things happened.

Devil worship. Human sacrifice. Animal mutilation. Witches' covens. Satanic cults that would kidnap your kids for their fiendish rituals.

Ranch 111 reportedly was an abandoned Scout camp. Today, it's home to a subdivision of homes, Firewheel Golf Course and One-Eleven Park in Garland. But before it was developed, Ranch 111 was a destination for thrill-seeking teens, who would pile into a car after dark and head there for a little adventure.

Sometimes they found more than they bargained on.

Susan Jantz remembers a nighttime foray with a group of friends out to Ranch 111 in the early 1980s—and a horrifying discovery.

"We saw several dead animals hanging in the tree, all bloody beyond recognition," she said. "I will never forget it!"

To add to the area's mystique, there was a big old oak tree that had been struck by lightning and grew sideways. Rumor had it that a few people had been hanged from the tree. Nearby was about ten acres of land where a Plano family, the Stovers, raised cattle and pigs. Sometime around 1977, devil worshippers allegedly carved up and bled out one of the family's steers.

"We actually saw a coven out there," one resident commented on Facebook. "I'm talking people in dark, hooded cloaks, chanting in a circle. It

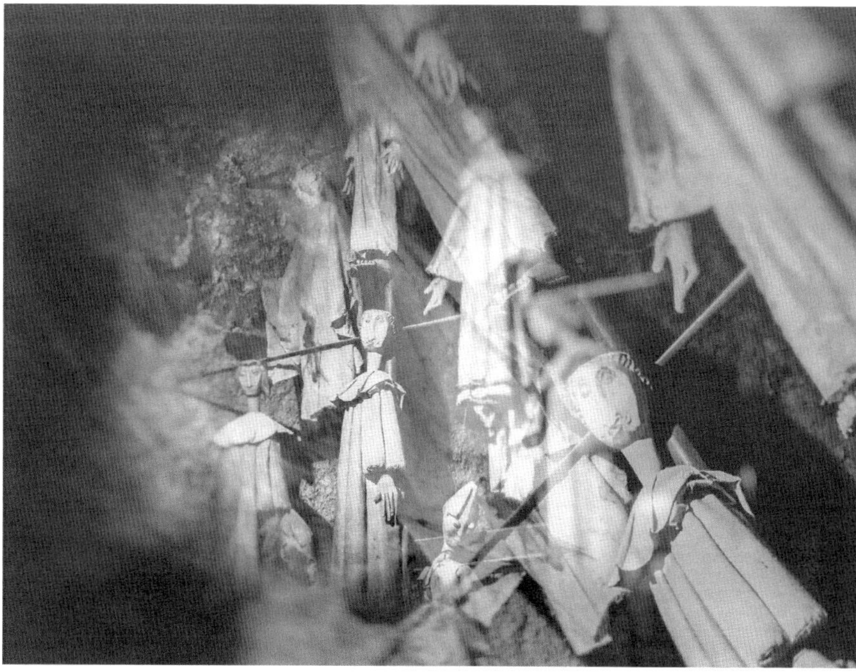

What really happened at Ranch 111? The truth is out there. *Shutterstock.*

scared the you-know-what right out of us." The group of friends took off at lightning speed and never returned.

One online forum on Ranch 111 drew ominous warnings from those who claimed to have witnessed its horrors. One called Ranch 111 "unholy ground" and pleaded with fellow forum members, "Please, don't go chasing horror stories. I did, and that decision cost me eight years of nasty experiences. Best to let some things lie."

Another reported a late-night visit when a man in a truck threatened him with a shotgun. They took off in a panic and crashed their car; the armed man left without stopping to see whether they needed help. One recalled some "distinctly weird" sights: a candle-like flame suspended in midair and multicolored lights that seemed to appear from nowhere.

Another in the forum observed a group of adults conducting a ritual around a bonfire. "I couldn't say whether this was a real hardcore satanic cult or if it was a bunch of young people sucked into the legend," he wrote. "I do know what I saw that night and it scared the hell out of me."

SCARY FUN

Longtime Plano resident Kenny Bush also confirmed multiple sightings of people dressed in black, gathered around bonfires. On one occasion, Kenny and his friend Carter Fitzgerald decided to take a group of girls to Ranch 111, partly to scare them and possibly to inspire a little romance. The kids all piled into Kenny's dad's old car.

Sure enough, they spotted a gathering of people in cloaks around a fire. When the girls started screaming, Kenny tore out through a pasture, hitting a rock and ripping a ten-inch gash in the gas tank. As gasoline poured out onto the road, the group inched home, terrified they'd end up stranded in this scary, isolated area where devil worshippers could turn up at any time. Luckily, they managed to make it back alive to a gas station and get the tank repaired.

"We could not get lucky with any of those beautiful women," Kenny joked. "Damn devil worshippers ruined it for us."

Not knowing of the place's reputation, another resident recalled going to Ranch 111 for a party, only to realize she'd actually been invited for a satanic ritual.

"Luckily, I left before they ate me," she said.

Another remembers visiting Ranch 111 to "have bonfires just to scare ourselves," she said. "Now it is a great park and we go out there for picnics with the whole family and dogs. Go figure."

THE SATANIC PANIC

Likely it's no coincidence that the legends swirling around Ranch 111 coincide with a period of mass media hysteria dubbed the "Satanic Panic," when many Americans were convinced that Satanists maintained a vast and unholy grip on society. At its height, it inspired a rash of false and often outlandish allegations of satanic ritual abuse in daycare centers in the 1980s.

A number of factors contributed to the Satanic Panic. First was the 1973 release of *The Exorcist*, one of the most profitable horror movies ever made. Loosely based on actual events, the story centered on a young girl, Regan (played by Linda Blair), who began levitating and speaking in tongues. After seeking medical help, to no avail, her mother turned to a local priest in desperation. The church sent in an expert to exorcise Regan's demons.

"*The Exorcist* profoundly impacted America's collective psyche regarding the existence of demons, and single-handedly transformed the popular Ouija board from a fun, harmless parlor game into a malevolent device capable of inducing spirit possession, demonic infestation, or other paranormal activity," wrote Aja Romano in a 2016 article for the website Vox.

Another factor was the 1969 publication of *The Satanic Bible* by Anton LaVey. A mishmash of mostly plagiarized ideas from writers like H.L. Mencken and Ayn Rand, the book became the key text for the Church of Satan, which LaVey founded in 1966. (The church still maintains a website, calling itself "the first above-ground organization in history openly dedicated to the acceptance of Man's true nature—that of a carnal beast, living in a cosmos that is indifferent to our existence.")

At the same time, Romano reported, Christian fundamentalism and a literal belief in angels and demons were on the rise, as were anti-occult crusaders like Pat Pulling, who claimed her son committed suicide due to a Dungeons and Dragons curse. Law enforcement jumped on the bandwagon, turning to self-styled "experts" in Satanism for guidance.

But what may have affected the public most deeply was the series of mass murders that put ritualistic killing in the headlines: the Manson murders in 1969, followed by the Zodiac Killer, Ted Bundy, John Wayne Gacy and David Berkowitz ("Son of Sam.") Not only did they commit horrific crimes, these killers also created a perception that they had an upper hand in some way. As Romano reported, "The Zodiac Killer and Berkowitz wrote taunting letters to the press and police; Bundy escaped from prison and immediately resumed his terrifying killing sprees; John Wayne Gacy hid his evil under the most banal of disguises, a friendly clown who performed for children."

Around the same time when the rumors of Ranch 111 began to spread in the 1970s and 1980s, the people of Plano likely had these fears—of the satanic, the occult and the demonic—on their minds. One remembers warnings in the news media issued at Halloween, cautioning parents to watch out for Satanists looking to kidnap their children.

At the same time, inspired by the hype, many young people dabbled in the occult. Mike Judge, creator of the animated TV series *King of the Hill* and a former resident of Richardson, poked fun at these wannabes in an episode titled "The Witches of East Arlen." (The episode features a coven led by a self-proclaimed warlock named Ward, who claims he's gifted with supernatural powers—but apparently not so powerful that he can escape his menial job at a video store or move out of his mother's basement.) No word on whether Mike Judge was inspired by the tales of Ranch 111, but it seems likely.

All of this is not to say that the reports of terrifying activity at Ranch 111 were imagined—only that the Satanic Panic may have been a self-fulfilling prophecy. Undoubtedly there were groups of people in dark cloaks who called themselves witches or Satanists and gathered at Ranch 111 late at night. But were they dangerous? For the most part, probably not.

19

The Witch Lady of Plano

If you grew up in Plano in the 1960s and 1970s, you probably knew about the "Witch Lady"—and you were afraid of her.

"She scared the Dickens out of us," as one longtime resident puts it.

As almost every southern gothic novel reminds us—a small town must have at least one truly eccentric character: someone with oddball habits, outlandish beliefs and, unfortunately, perhaps a few mental health issues. Vera Blanche Edens fit the bill on all counts.

Vera wore odd dark clothing. She wrote outrageous letters to the editor. She was a student of Nostradamus and ancient Phoenician literature. She didn't just tell trespassing youngsters to get off her lawn—she went after them with a weapon.

And it wasn't just kids who were leery of her. It turns out the FBI had a file on the Witch Lady of Plano.

Facebook Comments

In the late '60s and early '70s, kids rode their bikes all over the downtown area, and for a few ornery ones, passing through the yard of the Witch Lady was an irresistible challenge.

"We juvenile delinquents would ride across the edge of her yard, and out she would come chasing us off with a broom or hoe in her hands, screaming at us," said Kenny Bush, who grew up in Plano.

Now in his fifties, Kenny became curious about the woman who had left such an impression. He posted a query on a Plano history Facebook page and did a little digging.

It turns out Vera Edens was born in 1891, married in 1917 but widowed at a fairly young age. Sometime in the 1920s or 1930s, she moved to her home at 1509 Avenue G, across from what is now the Cox Building, and lived there, alone, until her death at age ninety in 1981. The house is gone now.

Vera is buried in Wylie Cemetery with her kin, who were early Collin County pioneers. Her grandfather was Elder Ezekiel Edens, who settled in Wylie in the mid-1800s. Her father, William Ely Edens, died in Allen in 1923.

On the Facebook page, Plano residents recalled that Vera displayed "witchcraft items" in her windows and sometimes wore long, black Eastern European–style clothing. Many recalled hearing stories about the Witch Lady from siblings or other kids. Some had no specific memories of her because, frightened, they had given her a wide berth.

"Her house was scary looking, dark and didn't seem to be a friendly place," one resident recalled. "I only saw her once on her front porch. I never wanted to get too close. I had heard too many stories. I had heard her called the 'Witch Lady,' and that was enough for me."

Another resident who worked in a title office had read Vera's will and said her probate records made for "interesting reading." Apparently, Vera mentioned several nieces and nephews by name, stating that she was leaving them nothing—because they were Christians.

A man who worked as a dispatcher at the Plano Police Department in the late '70s remembered many calls coming from the Witch Lady. Occasionally, there were calls about her, too. It may be that dementia set in in her later years, because at times she would leave the house without remembering to get dressed.

LANGUAGE KEY

Vera read widely and held some unconventional beliefs—and loved publicity.

In 1949, she claimed to have discovered a key in ancient Phoenician literature that enabled her to understand any language. Somehow, she managed to interest an Associated Press reporter in her claim, and the story was published in multiple newspapers.

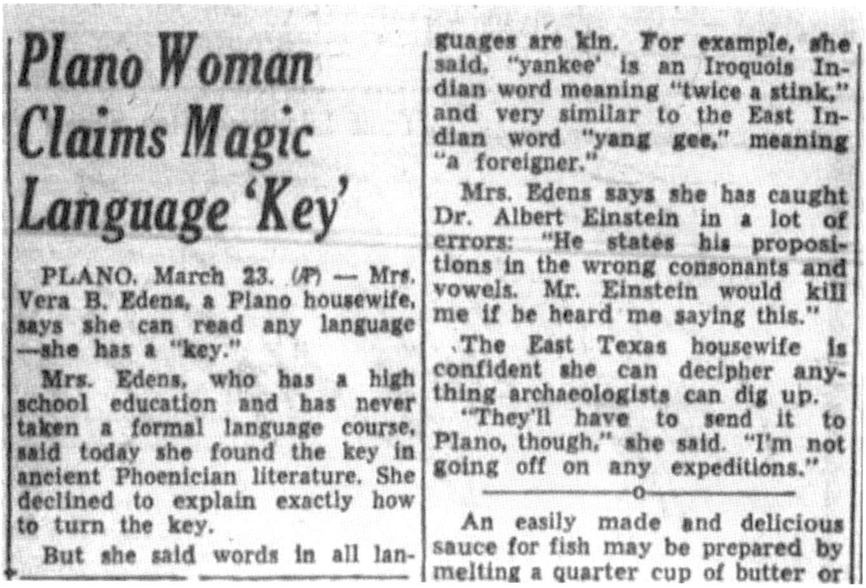

Plano Woman Claims Magic Language 'Key'

PLANO, March 23. (AP) — Mrs. Vera B. Edens, a Plano housewife, says she can read any language —she has a "key."

Mrs. Edens, who has a high school education and has never taken a formal language course, said today she found the key in ancient Phoenician literature. She declined to explain exactly how to turn the key.

But she said words in all languages are kin. For example, she said, "yankee' is an Iroquois Indian word meaning "twice a stink," and very similar to the East Indian word "yang gee," meaning "a foreigner."

Mrs. Edens says she has caught Dr. Albert Einstein in a lot of errors: "He states his propositions in the wrong consonants and vowels. Mr. Einstein would kill me if he heard me saying this."

The East Texas housewife is confident she can decipher anything archaeologists can dig up.

"They'll have to send it to Plano, though," she said. "I'm not going off on any expeditions."

An easily made and delicious sauce for fish may be prepared by melting a quarter cup of butter or

Associated Press story on Vera Edens's "discovery." *Newspapers.com.*

"I challenge anyone to write anything in any language that I can't understand," she said in the article. "As long as it isn't nonsense."

The article stated that the "Plano housewife" had "declined to explain exactly how to turn the key." The article also noted that Vera had "caught Dr. Albert Einstein in a number of errors."

Vera also loved a good fight. Apparently, she sued Twentieth Century Fox, claiming plagiarism in the 1945 film *Where Do We Go from Here?* starring Fred MacMurray and June Haver. Vera accused the studio of stealing the story from a scenario she wrote titled "Hunters of the Promise Land." After a judge dismissed the case, Vera tried again; the case was dismissed the second time with prejudice—she could not sue again.

Vera's name also turns up occasionally in articles in the *Plano Star-Courier*, which described her as the historian of the "Hage-Naut Religious Order." (That's possibly a misspelling; Google turns up nothing on that group.) She was also associated with the Richardson Unitarian Church.

In one altercation, covered in the paper, Vera became upset at the adjoining property owner, who was erecting a fence down the property line. Vera claimed the fence was three feet onto her property and threatened the fence builder with an axe.

She often wrote letters to the editor at the *Dallas Morning News* and the *Plano Star-Courier*, which the papers would occasionally publish. In one 1951 letter, she expressed her admiration for Nostradamus, asserting that his book, *Centuries by Measure*, had come true so far. When the paper inserted a few words of explanation, calling Nostradamus an "astrologer," she took issue in a second, scolding letter, insisting that he was "an astronomer, a Euclid scholar and a doctor of medicine" as well as a "prophet of the stars."

Another letter, in the *Star-Courier*, complained about the sheep in the nativity scene at the First Christian Church. Her beef? Apparently, an astrological "discovery" convinced her that the sign of the sheep was no longer relevant.

"Why has no one ever told the Christian 'goons' that we are now in the 2,000-year age of the 2-Fishes, Sign of the Feet, and have been out of the Aries Age of Ram Sheep Lamb since then?" she griped.

THE WITCH LADY'S FBI FILE

Like many other eccentric characters, Vera Edens had her own conspiracy theory about John F. Kennedy's assassination. But hers was concerning enough that the FBI opened up a file, FBI Evidence DL 100-10461.

According to the file, Vera had sent a letter to a company "engaged in religious advertising" called Coleman Advertising Service, and owner Jim Coleman decided to contact the FBI. Apparently, the letter was laced with anti-Semitic comments as well as her theory about the assassination:

> *Lee Oswald did not kill John Kennedy. He only shot at General Walker to try to show he MEANT TO KILL HIM when he agreed with the CIA and the Kennedys to do so. He never meant to kill him. Marina Oswald told that Lee told her he shot at Gen. Walker…this to The World, to vindicate her husband's honor THE BEST SHE KNEW HOW. She wanted the CIA to know Lee kept his word to kill Walker. Oh, what's the use in opening your mouth….THE WHOLE DAMN WORLD is gone crazy. Minds are as blank as the day you were born.*

The file goes on to say that Edens had been publishing material, "anti-Jewish and anti-United Nations," since 1950.

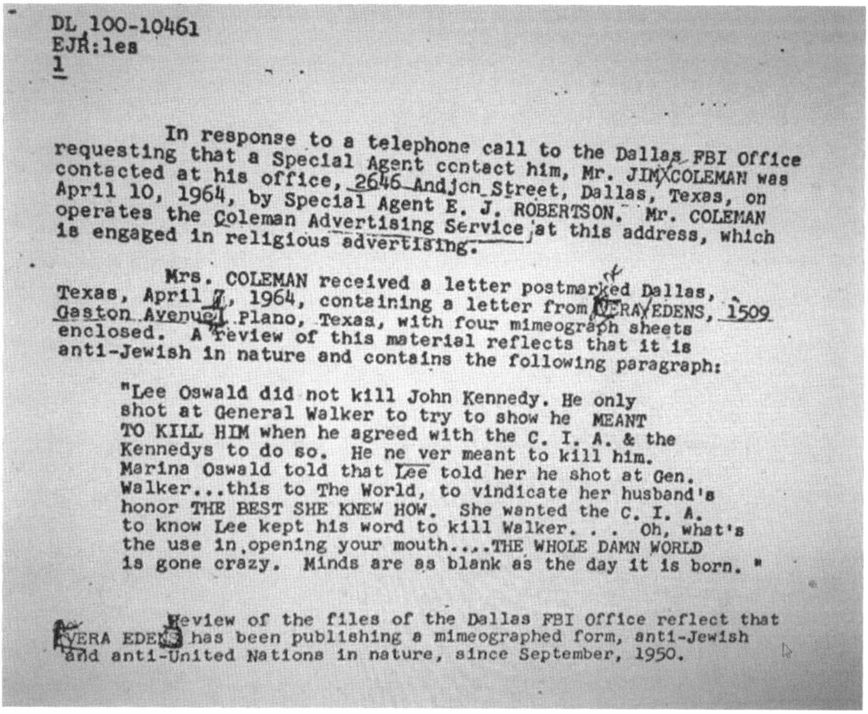

DL 100-10461
EJR:les
1

In response to a telephone call to the Dallas FBI Office requesting that a Special Agent contact him, Mr. JIM COLEMAN was contacted at his office, 2646 Andjon Street, Dallas, Texas, on April 10, 1964, by Special Agent E. J. ROBERTSON. Mr. COLEMAN operates the Coleman Advertising Service at this address, which is engaged in religious advertising.

Mrs. COLEMAN received a letter postmarked Dallas, Texas, April 7, 1964, containing a letter from VERA EDENS, 1509 Gaston Avenue, Plano, Texas, with four mimeograph sheets enclosed. A review of this material reflects that it is anti-Jewish in nature and contains the following paragraph:

"Lee Oswald did not kill John Kennedy. He only shot at General Walker to try to show he MEANT TO KILL HIM when he agreed with the C. I. A. & the Kennedys to do so. He ne ver meant to kill him. Marina Oswald told that Lee told her he shot at Gen. Walker...this to The World, to vindicate her husband's honor THE BEST SHE KNEW HOW. She wanted the C. I. A. to know Lee kept his word to kill Walker. . . Oh, what's the use in opening your mouth....THE WHOLE DAMN WORLD is gone crazy. Minds are as blank as the day it is born."

Review of the files of the Dallas FBI Office reflect that VERA EDENS has been publishing a mimeographed form, anti-Jewish and anti-United Nations in nature, since September, 1950.

The Witch Lady's FBI file. *Courtesy of Kenny Bush.*

Some residents on the Facebook page expressed regrets about tormenting the Witch Lady with pranks. Today, Vera's neighbors might be more empathetic. We're more aware of mental health issues. Medication may have helped.

But we can also thank Vera Edens for giving those who grew up in Plano the colorful tale of the Witch Lady of Plano to reminisce over, many years later.

IV

Dark Moments in Plano History

20
The Night Watchman

Author's note:

There are rumors that Deputy City Marshal Green Wesley Rye still haunts the back alleys and shadowy corners of downtown Plano, but I could not find any firsthand accounts to confirm. I did, however, have the privilege of meeting a Plano Police officer who was so haunted by Rye's story that he felt compelled to learn what really happened on the fateful night of February 28, 1920, when G.W. Rye was killed by a group of bank robbers. Thanks to his research, Rye's sacrifice is not forgotten.

On cold winter evenings, almost one hundred years ago, Green Wesley Rye strolled the streets and back alleys of downtown Plano. While his official title was deputy city marshal, Officer Rye acted as a night watchman. He was a solitary figure, carrying a lantern and big brass key. The key acted as a sort of timecard; Rye inserted it into time clocks located at the doorways of business establishments as he made his rounds.

His job was critical to the safety of Plano's citizens. While the railroads brought business and goods into Plano, they also brought crime. Hobos riding the rails would sometimes travel from town to town, jumping off to rob a bank or burglarize a shop and then jumping back on the next train.

For most of his shift, Officer Rye was alone, but he did occasionally pause to chat or share a cup of coffee with the town baker, J.J. Vavra, who owned

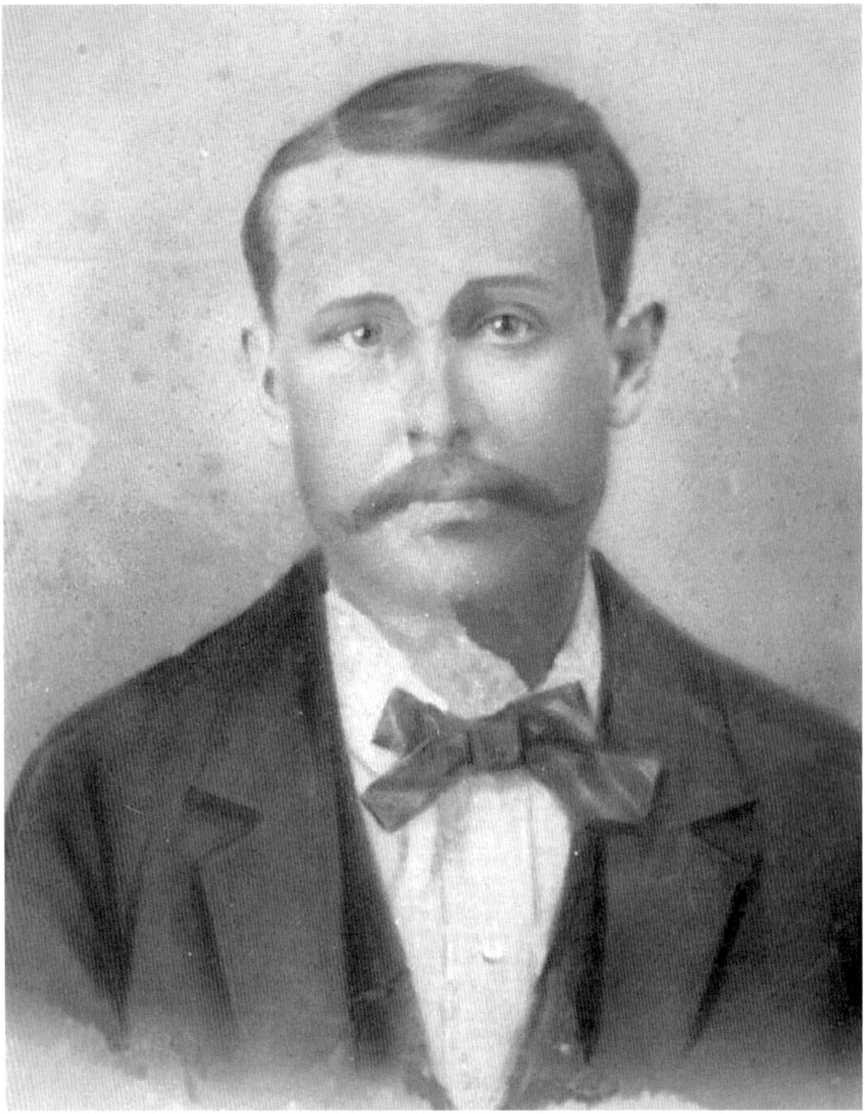

Deputy Marshal Green Wesley Rye. *Courtesy of the Plano Police Department.*

the Blue Ribbon Bakery in Plano. Vavra and his wife were up early to start the ovens and begin the baking.

Early in the morning of February 28, 1920, at 4:45 a.m., Officer Rye clocked in at the Plano National Bank (currently the A.R. Schell Building) on what is now Fifteenth Street. Suddenly, he was surprised by a group of yeggs just as they were attempting to escape with loot stolen from the bank's vault. ("Yegg" was a 1920s slang term for a burglar or safecracker.)

Shots rang out. Officer Rye was hit once in the abdomen and managed to return fire before collapsing. He was taken to Vavra's home but soon succumbed to his injury. By the time his wife and three children arrived, it was too late. His last words, according to a newspaper report, were, "My poor wife, my poor children." The yeggs got away with money and valuables in safe deposit boxes, worth about $140,000.

And then, Plano promptly forgot about Deputy City Marshal Green Wesley Rye.

History Uncovered

For decades, Plano Police officers believed that no one of their ranks had ever died in the line of duty. There was no memorial plaque for a fallen officer in Plano Police headquarters. There was no Plano officer's name inscribed on the Texas Peace Officers Memorial in Austin or listed in the National Law Enforcement Officers Memorial.

Officer Rye's death merited just a short mention in a Plano history book published in the 1950s. When that blurb caught the eye of Detective Luke Grant, a Plano Police officer since 1983, he was intrigued.

Officer Grant, a history and genealogy buff, decided to do a little detective work to learn more. He visited libraries in Plano, McKinney, Dallas and Durant, Oklahoma, and combed through history books and microfilms of old newspapers.

He learned that Rye, fifty-two, had served with the Plano Police Department for eighteen months when he was felled by a .45-caliber bullet from a handgun. To his surprise, one newspaper article described Officer Rye as a sworn officer with a badge, a gun and full arrest powers.

That was an important discovery.

"Because most accounts referred to Rye as a night watchman, everyone had assumed that he was a security guard," said Officer Grant. But as a sworn officer, Rye was a "brother in blue"—an officer who had died in the line of duty, someone whose memory would be honored by fellow officers, in Plano and beyond.

Soon, Officer Grant had solved one mystery: Why had Officer Rye's death been so quickly overlooked in Plano?

First, Rye was one of just two men who comprised law enforcement in Plano, which was a small town in 1920. The other man left the force within a year. Also, Rye's widow and children left Plano immediately after his death. He was buried in San Saba, Texas, and the family stayed there, never returning to Plano. His funeral notice in the local newspaper noted he was a member of San Saba's Baptist church, "a good man and citizen…who lived and labored in San Saba for a number of years and had many friends here."

Finding the Family

But Officer Grant needed more proof than a newspaper clipping to have Officer Rye's name added to state and national memorials for fallen officers. He tracked down Rye's granddaughter Molly Lane in Austin. When they connected by telephone, she became emotional. She told Officer Grant that she'd inherited her grandfather's tin badge.

Officer Grant held his breath as he asked her to read the inscription on the badge.

"Police, Plano, Texas," Molly said. That was the missing piece of evidence needed to prove that Rye was a lawman.

Molly shared how her grandfather's death had traumatized the family and how she had attempted to get the state to acknowledge her grandfather's sacrifice, with no luck. Her mother, who was ten when her father was killed, relived that fateful morning from time to time until her death at age ninety-one in 2000. As Molly told the *Dallas Morning News*, "Every time a police officer got killed, she'd come to me and say, 'They've killed my daddy. They've killed my daddy.'…It just messed with her head."

Officer Grant and Police Chief Greg Rushin traveled to Austin to visit the family and pay their respects. Molly graciously donated the badge, and another family member donated Rye's pistol. They shared family photos, which Officer Grant added to the stuffed, three-inch notebook in which he carefully filed the records and notes related to the case.

Molly also gave him a copy of Rye's funeral notice in the San Saba newspaper, which closed with these poignant words: "Whether he was shot from ambush and then discharged his own pistol to alarm the people and call for help, or whether he was engaged in an effort to stop the bold robbers will likely remain a mystery as he was unable to tell the story after assistance came to him. But in either case, Green Wesley Rye died like a brave man doing his duty."

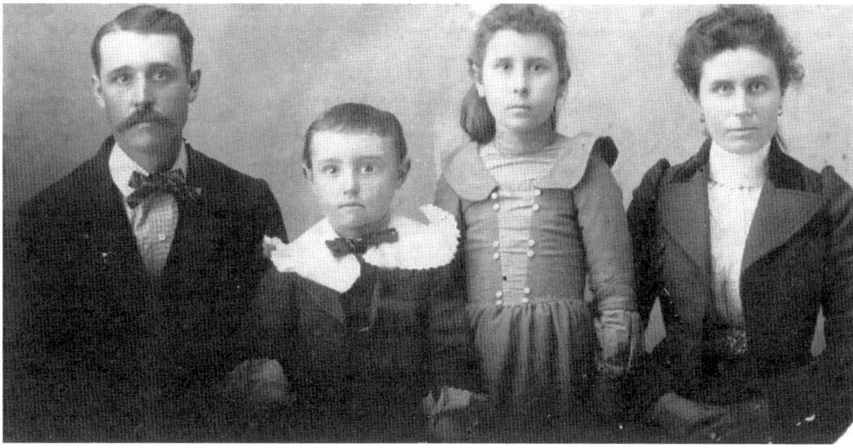

Officer Rye and his family. *Courtesy of the Plano Police Department.*

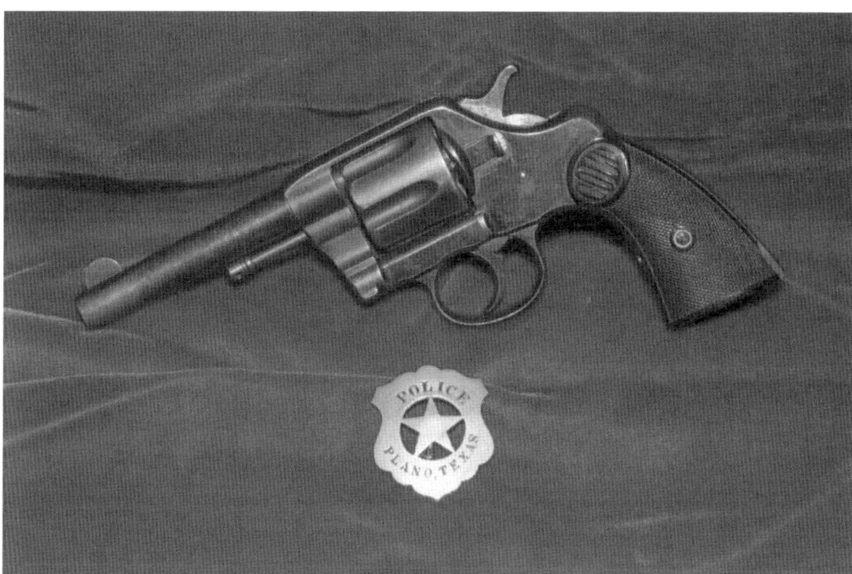

Officer Rye's badge and pistol. *Courtesy of the Plano Police Department.*

Cold Case

When he started his research, Officer Grant initially began looking through newspapers in 1921 because of an error—he'd simply written down the wrong year in his notes. He calls that mistake a "God moment"—a bit of divine intervention that helped him uncover more information, previously forgotten, about who killed Officer Rye.

Newspaper articles in March 1921 said that Dallas's chief of detectives and the Collin County sheriff had traveled to a city jail in Durant, Oklahoma, to question a man who confessed to taking part in a bank robbery in Plano.

Now Officer Grant was presented with a tantalizing possibility. Could he solve the cold case of who murdered Green Wesley Rye more than eighty years earlier?

Officer Grant traveled to Durant to pore through prison records and files of the Durant newspaper. He learned that the man, Alfred Gonia, was a career criminal who confessed he was one of four men and a woman who had robbed the Plano National Bank. Gonia claimed he was just the lookout—he hadn't killed anyone, just fired a few warning shots. He had collected $1,300 (equivalent to about $16,000 in 2018) from the heist.

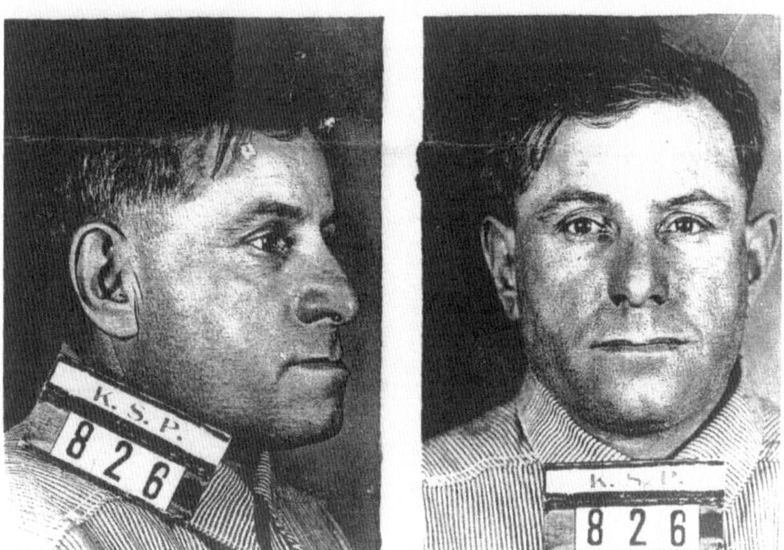

Alfred Gonia, the man Luke Grant believes killed Green Wesley Rye. *Courtesy of the Plano Police Department.*

But during a break from questioning, Gonia attempted to kill himself, using a sharpened spoon to cut his own throat. After that, he would never discuss the burglary again. Officer Grant traced Gonia's prison career until 1934, when he was released from the Kansas Penitentiary. And then the trail goes cold.

We'll probably never get a definitive answer about who killed Green Wesley Rye, Officer Grant said, but "I believe in my heart that Gonia is the shooter."

Surprise Witness

There was one more surprise in store for Officer Grant.

On February 27, 2003, almost exactly eighty-three years after Rye's death, the *Dallas Morning News* ran a story about Officer Grant's detective work and Officer Rye's sacrifice, with the headline: "The Lawman That History Forgot." The article concluded with a plea from Officer Grant for anyone with information about the case to call, with a telephone number.

Someone did call. Officer Grant received a phone call from an elderly woman named Anna May Shaw.

"I guess you didn't figure you'd hear from an eyewitness," she said.

Anna May, age eighty-eight, was the daughter of J.J. Vavra, the baker, and was just four years old when Rye was killed.

She recalled how her mother had heard the shots and, fearing her husband had been robbed, grabbed a pistol. Her mother saw two men running across the railroad tracks and shot at them, but missed.

Anna May also remembered vividly how Rye's body was carried into the bedroom in her parent's house. His eyes were still open, but he didn't move, which had confused her.

"I can't remember what I ate for breakfast today, but I can still remember that scene as if it happened yesterday," she told Grant.

In the Line of Duty

Rye remained the only Plano officer lost in the line of duty until July 7, 2007, when Officer Dayle Weston (Wes) Hardy was killed in a traffic accident.

Now, every year, Plano Police hold a ceremony honoring the city's two fallen officers: Traffic Officer Wes Hardy and Deputy City Marshal Green Wesley Rye—one of recent memory, and the other almost one hundred years ago, whose story was almost lost to us.

Today, Green Wesley Rye is far from forgotten. Thanks to Detective Grant's research, a plaque commemorating his sacrifice was installed across the street from the A.R. Schell Building on Fifteenth Street—the same building that once housed the Plano National Bank. Some of Rye's descendants traveled to Plano for the installation.

Every February 28, the Plano Police dispatcher announces an "End of Watch," and members of the force pause to remember Officer Rye. Each class of new Plano Police Department recruits completes the "Green Wesley Rye Memorial Run," a two-mile trek that takes the soon-to-be officers past the spot where Rye was shot.

If you visit the Plano Police department's headquarters, you'll see a portrait on the wall honoring Rye—the first Plano law enforcement officer to die in the line of duty. Rye's name is inscribed in the memorial in Austin.

There's also a page honoring Rye on a national website, the "Officer Down Memorial Page: Remembering All of Law Enforcement's Heroes."

There, visitors can post words of reflections. The comments on Officer Rye's page serve as poignant reminders of the kinship that police officers share with their brothers and sisters in blue—even one lost almost one hundred years ago.

"Your watch has ended but the memory of your service remains. Rest in Peace my brother," wrote a Plano Police officer.

Another officer offered this poem, author unknown, imagining a police officer standing before God on judgment day:

Step forward now, Officer. You've borne your burdens well.
Come walk a beat on heaven's streets.
You've done your time in hell.

Plano salutes you, Officer Hardy and Officer Rye. May your sacrifices never be forgotten.

21

Plano's Darkest Hour

The Smallpox Epidemic

Today, Preston Lakes is a quiet, manicured neighborhood in an affluent area of Plano. Almost 120 years ago, it was the site of one of Plano's darkest hours.

Imagine two men working under cover of darkness on an isolated patch of farmland. They toiled at night, believing that would reduce the chance of infection. Their grim task: burying the body of an eleven-year-old girl, a member of the Collinsworth family.

The men weren't just grieving. They were terrified. Who would die next?

The little girl was the first victim in a smallpox outbreak that ultimately killed fifteen and rocked the community of Plano in 1895.

"It was a scary time," said Charlotte Carpenter Johnson, an Allen resident and descendant of the family. "They had to bury the dead very quickly."

Killer Hospitality

The sad saga began days earlier, when, following frontier custom, the family of Daniel M. "Milt" Collinsworth welcomed a traveling peddler into the home.

"Unfortunately, the family's hospitality ended up being their demise," said Plano preservation advocate Candace Fountoulakis.

At the time, Plano was a small community of just 1,300 souls; the extended Collinsworth family owned large portions of what is now west

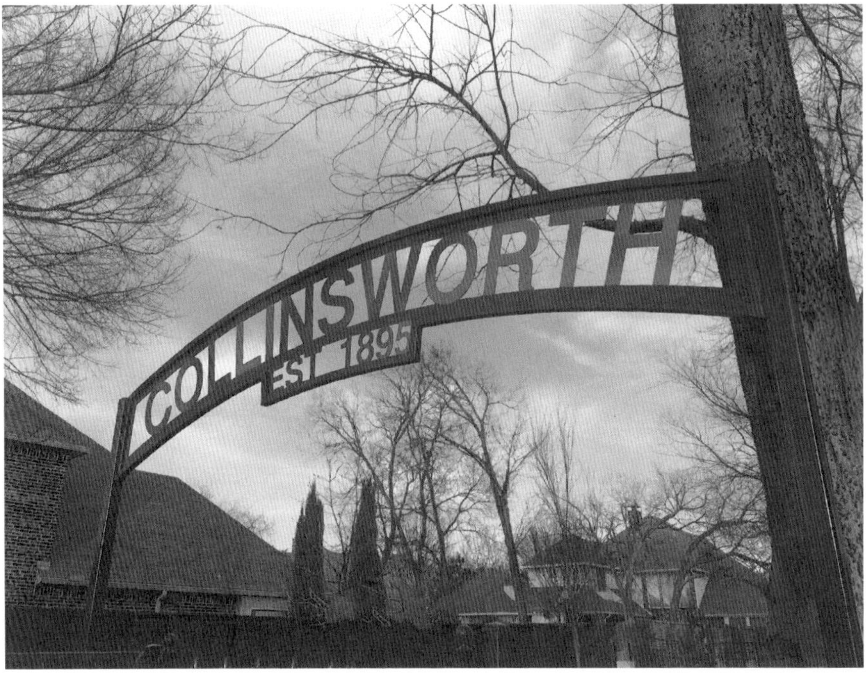

Entrance to Collinsworth Cemetery, created during the smallpox outbreak. *Photo by the author.*

Plano. They were farmers from Tennessee and Virginia and relatives of James Collinsworth, a signer of the Texas Declaration of Independence.

When the peddler left the next morning, he mentioned that he felt unwell. The chore of changing his bed linens fell to one of Milt's daughters. Within a few days, she fell ill. Inexperienced with the disease, the community's doctor misdiagnosed her ailment.

Family members traveled from Allen and Frisco for the funeral. It was a dreary, rainy day, so mourners crowded into the home, with the windows shut. Silently, the deadly disease spread.

Charlotte is the great-great-granddaughter of Farwick Collinsworth, the family patriarch.

"Within a matter of weeks," she said, "Farwick lost his wife, two sons, a nephew and at least three grandchildren."

Farwick's wife, Lucy Ann Collinsworth, sixty-four, died next, followed by two of their sons, Levi, thirty-seven, and Ishmel, twenty-five, and two more grandchildren, Mary, three, and Robert, ten. Tobe Collinsworth, twenty-three, a nephew visiting from Kentucky, also died. Other names are lost to

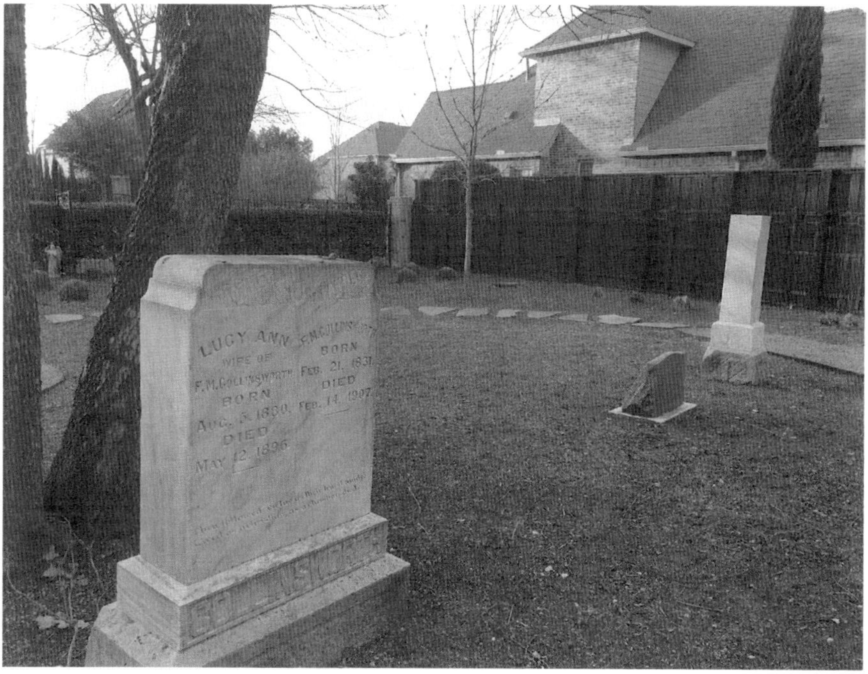

A headstone at Collinsworth Cemetery. *Photo by the author.*

history, but Charlotte, who researched the Collinsworth family extensively, believes about fifteen ultimately perished.

McKinney's newspaper, the *Democrat*, printed a resolution by the Collin County Alliance, expressing sympathy: "The family of Brother F.M. Collinsworth of Haggard Alliance have been terribly afflicted by the visitation of smallpox in his family resulting in the death of several family members....Therefore, be it resolved that we tender to the surviving members our heartfelt sympathy in their sore bereavement."

ARMED QUARANTINE

Settlers in the area quickly realized that they needed to do more than extend sympathy. They needed to take action to stop the spread of disease.

On May 6, 1895, city council called an emergency meeting, requiring vaccinations and establishing a strict quarantine "to protect our citizens from

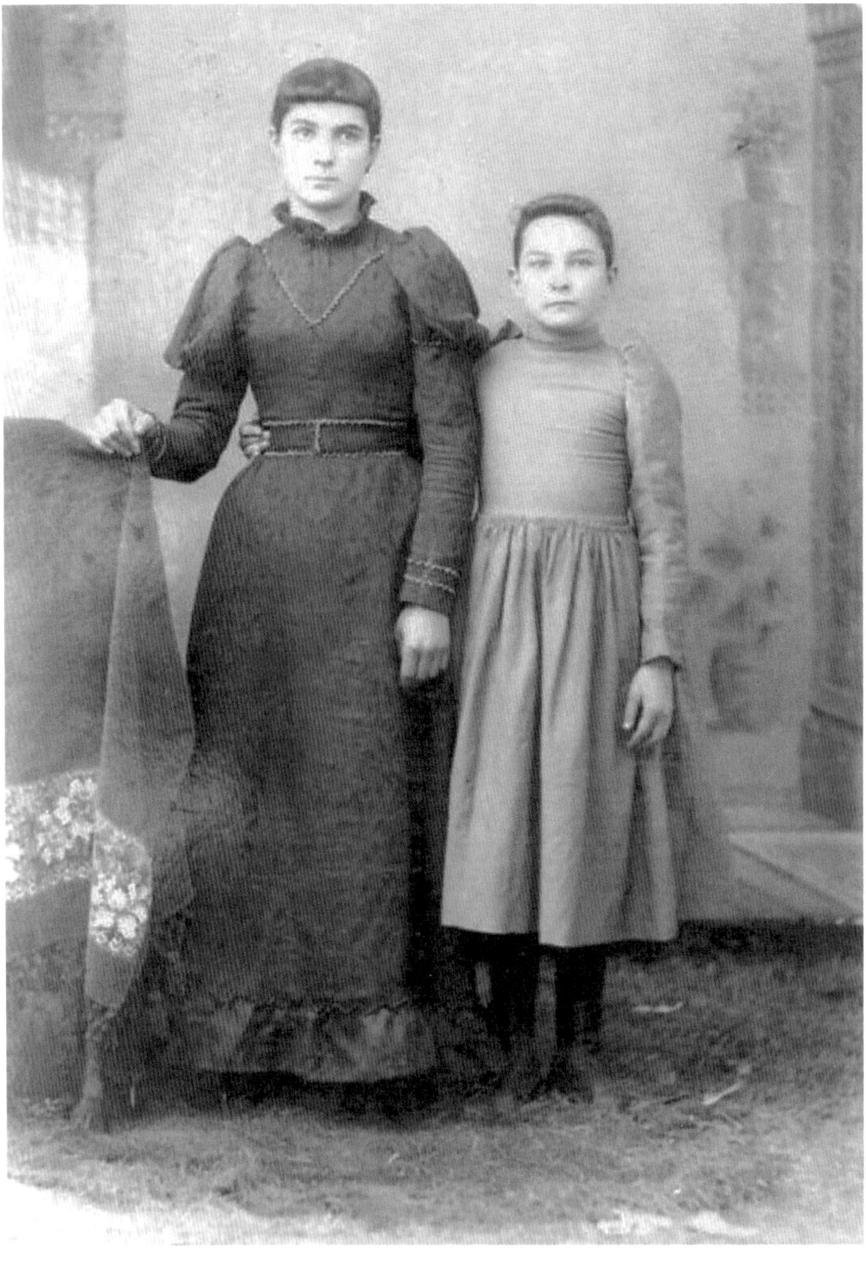

Annie Collinsworth and her sister. *Courtesy of Charlotte Carpenter Johnson.*

this loathsome disease." Anyone within the area between what is now Spring Creek Parkway, Park Boulevard, Coit and Preston Roads was forbidden to leave. An armed guard patrolled the border.

For those within the quarantine, food supplies were limited. One survivor, a man named Bob Fortner, later vowed that he'd never eat rice again, having relied on it for so many meals during this time.

A few brave souls endeavored to assist. One smallpox survivor, Albert Garrett, nursed the sick. Silas Harrington, owner of a pharmacy downtown, delivered groceries to the quarantine line.

History leaves us no details on the traveling salesman, but he likely was part of a chain of transmission that had gradually carried the disease toward Plano. An epidemic had ravaged Brooklyn, New York, from 1892 to 1894, triggering panic and riots. Patients with smallpox experience a sudden onset of high fever, malaise, headaches, body aches and sometimes vomiting. The rash does not appear until after two to four days, which may explain the doctor's initial misdiagnosis of the Collinsworth girl.

A Peaceful Monument

Oddly, Charlotte never heard about the epidemic until stumbling across a newspaper article. She thinks the memory was too painful for the family.

"The Collinsworth family had a stigma on them for many years afterward," she said. "Their neighbors were frightened and avoided them."

Happily, however, the story concludes on a note of healing. The outbreak established Collinsworth Cemetery, which now occupies a quiet spot between two homes near Parker and Ohio Roads. Once forgotten, it now occupies a beautifully landscaped lot in the neighborhood.

When Charlotte learned of the graveyard's existence in the late 1980s, it was in disrepair. But one by one, community groups stepped in to help. Toll Brothers provided the fence, the Fulbright family donated the entrance sign and Plano Conservancy added a wayside marker. Preston Lakes HOA, Boy Scouts and master gardeners pitched in with landscaping and other projects. Charlotte formed a 501c nonprofit association to manage the property. (The family owns the graveyard in perpetuity.)

"It was really an amazing cooperative effort," she said. "I couldn't begin to list all of the people who have helped."

When the development opened, some of the first buyers in the area opted for properties right next door to the cemetery. As they saw it, they were getting a home next to a park—and neighbors they could count on to be very quiet.

Now, anyone can enjoy the serene spot and visit the graves of Lucy, Ishmel and Levy, whose headstone calls him "a loving husband, a dear father, a faithful friend."

"The cemetery went from being a swampy, muddy mess…to a beautiful place of renewal and hope," said Fountoulakis. "I think that's exactly how the family would want it to be represented."

About Smallpox

Prior to the wide availability of the vaccine, smallpox was one of the most feared diseases on the planet. It was extremely contagious and killed and disfigured millions. A 1988 article in the *American Journal of Public Health* described the havoc wreaked by this horrific disease:

> *Imagine what it would be like if you could get AIDS by simply standing near an infected person at work, in school, in a hospital or anywhere else; if you had a chance of dying of one in four if you did get it….Imagine that when you did contract the disease it would transform you into a hideous monster, rack your body with constant pain, and cause your family and friends to fear and shun you—some perceiving your illness as evidence of divine wrath.*[13]

Tragically, Plano's outbreak occurred almost one hundred years after Edward Jenner discovered the smallpox vaccine in 1796. (Jenner never made a profit; he chose not to patent the vaccine, because he believed it should be available for all.) The smallpox vaccination was introduced in the United States in 1800, however, for the Collinsworth family and others on the frontier, it likely wasn't easy to obtain.

Some were fearful or suspicious of the vaccine. While it was effective in reducing the spread of disease, state-imposed vaccination programs met with resistance from the beginning.

The pioneers likely contracted the *variola major* type, with a fatality rate of 20 to 50 percent, according to Daphne Lynch, an epidemiologist with

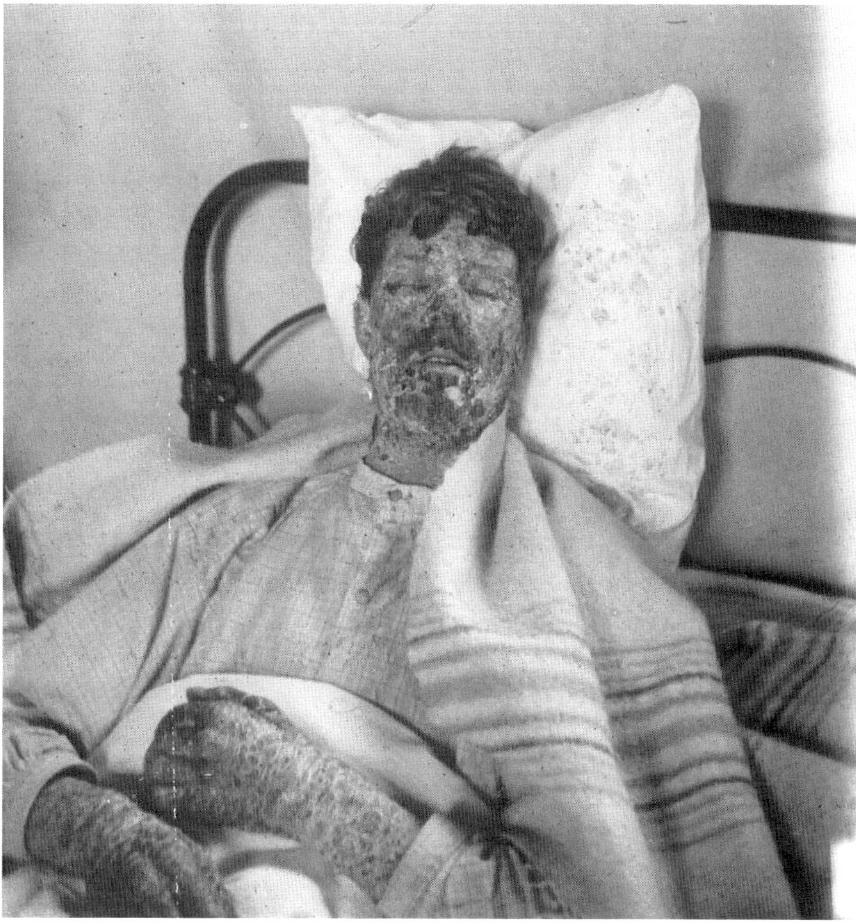

Edward Davis, a smallpox victim during the 1895–96 outbreak in Gloucester, England. *Wikimedia Commons.*

Collin County Health Care Services. Even those who survived suffered for the rest of their lives. Some were blinded. Young women whose faces were horribly disfigured found their marriage prospects evaporate overnight. Some committed suicide or entered convents.

In 1895, the year smallpox struck Plano, two major milestones in the disease's history also occurred. They illustrate how disparities in the adoption of the vaccine became a matter of life and death. Sweden, the first country to adopt Jenner's vaccine, announced the eradication of smallpox in that country in 1895. The same year, the town of Gloucester, England, was struck by a smallpox epidemic that ultimately killed 434 people.

England had required vaccination for all babies since 1853, but that law sparked the world's first anti-vaccination societies, publications and rallies. "The state has no right to encroach upon parental responsibility, or to impose either religious or medical dogmas upon the people of this country on any pretense whatever," wrote William Tebb, president of the London Society for the Abolition of Compulsory Vaccination, in 1887.[14]

A wave of anti-vaxx feeling took root in Gloucester, with several officials elected for their opposition of "Jennerism" and their promises not to prosecute those who opted out of vaccination. Gloucester became the least-vaccinated county in the country, with 83 percent of the population failing to comply with the law. Then the horror began. Perhaps because of the political debate, many photographs still exist documenting the terrible effects of the disease.

A mass vaccination effort ultimately put the outbreak under control, but not before almost two thousand people were infected, two-thirds of them children under age ten. The Gloucester outbreak—which, ironically, took place less than twenty miles from the spot where Jenner developed the vaccine—was Britain's last great smallpox epidemic.

Smallpox was declared eradicated in 1979 by the World Health Organization. Until 2018, no treatment was available, other than vaccination.

22

The Muncey Incident

The Gruesome Fate of Plano's First Settlers

On a recent sunny morning, students at Collin College strolled across campus and sipped coffee in the atrium. None stopped to read the small historic marker in front of the admissions office. Most seemed oblivious to the horrific murders that occurred nearby in Plano's earliest days—taking the lives of at least five people and striking "cold fear into the hearts of the early settlers," a fear that haunted them for years to come.

According to newspaper and other accounts, William Rice, his son and Leonard Searcy and his son set out on a hunting trip along Rowlett Creek one day late in 1844. Leonard Searcy peeled off from the hunting party to visit the Munceys, who were living in a temporary shelter near Rowlett Creek. It was there that "a most terrible and heartrending sight met his startled vision."

Jeremiah Muncey and McBain Jameson had been shot in the head. The Munceys' small child, about two or three years of age, had been beaten to death, its head apparently bashed against a wall. Mrs. Muncey's breasts were cut off, and her body mutilated "in a most shocking manner" that newspaper accounts found too horrific to detail. It appeared she had tried to fight off the attackers with a Bowie knife, to no avail.

Blood had splashed on the walls of the camp. The family's feather beds had been ripped apart; feathers were scattered everywhere.

Apparently, the attack had taken place just a few hours before. The Munceys' three sons were nowhere to be seen.

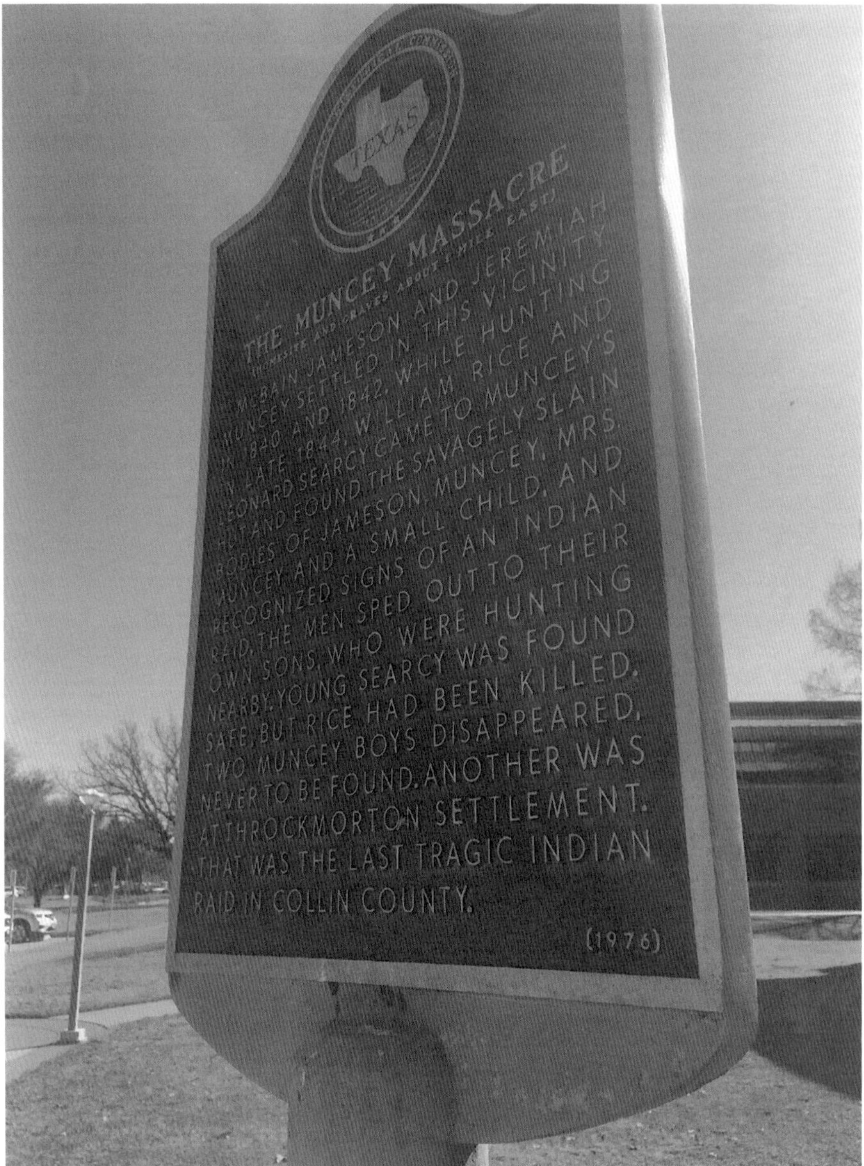

Historical marker for the Muncey incident. *Photo by the author.*

Searcy quickly returned to his hunting party to warn the others. When he arrived, only the elder Rice was at the camp; the two sons had ridden off to hunt. The men immediately went searching for them and soon found the mutilated body of Rice's son. They loaded his body on one of their horses and headed to their homes near Wilson's Creek, about ten miles away. At home, they found Searcy's son, who had managed to escape.

Young Searcy reported that he and the Rice boy had been surprised by a band of Indians. The Indians held up a white flag and motioned the boys to come near, and then several advanced, laying down their guns. The Searcy boy urged his companion not to allow the Indians to get too close, but then one of the Indians seized Rice's horse by the bridle. The Searcy boy managed to escape, but Rice was dragged from his bridle and scalped.

A party of men was gathered to follow the Indians, but they traveled too fast to be overtaken.

Later, one of Muncey's sons, age fifteen, turned up alive—he had left the family before the attack to go to another settlement for provisions. The other two Muncey boys, ages seventeen and twelve, were likely taken captive and never seen again. Human remains found along the trail later were believed to be those of the two boys.

An Impassioned Response

Oral history attributes the Muncey attack to Indians, based on the young Searcy's account and evidence at the scene. Indian raids did occur during this time in the North Texas area. Not surprisingly, the promise of free land that brought Anglo settlers to the area also resulted in conflicts with Indians. Their way of life was threatened by the settlers' arrival.

Some historians believe a party of Comanche may have passed through the area and perpetrated the raid. Around this time, members of the Caddo, Cherokee, Delaware, Kickapoo and Tonkawa tribes lived in the area. These tribes farmed and hunted in the area and, for the most part, coexisted peacefully with the settlers. Comanche, however, were warriors who engaged whites as well as other tribes in violent encounters.

In 2005, the *Dallas Morning News* published a historic account of the Muncey incident and, shortly after, printed an impassioned response from Peggy Larney, a representative of the Indian (now more commonly known as Native American) community in North Texas.

Larney called the article "badly biased and one-sided" and noted, correctly, that there were no eyewitnesses to the killing of Jameson and the Muncey family. She questioned the creation of a historical marker that "casually blamed Indians when our people could truthfully claim so many more 'massacre memories' than you could ever imagine?"

Her op-ed does offer one important reminder: at the time, settlers had no access to forensics or, for that matter, any sort of professional law enforcement. While the settlers' accounts do point to an Indian raid, that's our only evidence.

A TESTAMENT TO DETERMINATION

According to the Plano Conservancy for Historic Preservation's history of the Muncey incident, "We will never know the true story of who was actually involved, for the telling of the story from generation to generation has likely introduced assumptions and biases that do not reflect the original event."

Perhaps the more important takeaway from the Munceys' story is this: life on the frontier was dangerous. Settlers were isolated and vulnerable—whether to human violence, to predator animals that roamed the area, to starvation or the elements. The influx of settlers continued even after this incident. It is a testament to the determination of Plano's earliest pioneers.

PLANO'S FIRST SETTLERS

McBain Jameson is believed to be Plano's first white settler, arriving in 1840. His friend Jeremiah Muncey and his family followed two years later. Both had been drawn to the area by the promise of free land, offered by the Republic of Texas to encourage settlements in unappropriated lands. Jameson received his first conditional certificate (land grant) from the Republic of Texas on January 2, 1840; Muncey received his on January 3, 1842.

The Muncey incident was long considered the last violent episode between settlers and American Indians in Collin County. A few encounters with Indians occurred later but did not result in violence.

Shortly after the incident, Texas became a state on December 28, 1845, and Collin became a county about a year later. But Plano was still sparsely populated in the 1840s and wasn't incorporated until almost thirty years later, in 1873.

Today, there are descendants of the Rice and Searcy families living in the area but no Muncey descendants. According to an inventory taken at the time, all that was left of the Muncey family was 440 acres of land, one axe and one set of wagon irons.

23

The Hanging of Stephen Ballew

Late in the spring of 1872, several of the men of Plano saddled up their horses and set out for McKinney. They were about to witness the first legal hanging in Collin County.

Facing execution was a man from Tennessee named Stephen Ballew, seventeen, reviled as "The Inhuman Murderer; the Expert Confidence Operator and the Monster Liar of His Age."[15] He'd been convicted of murdering James Golden, thirty, about three miles outside of McKinney. Collin County sheriff William Nelson Bush, a Plano resident, helped bring him to justice.

The circumstances of the murder were shocking. People on the frontier relied on hospitality and neighborly cooperation to survive. Ballew had cruelly betrayed a family in Illinois that had taken him in.

Posing as a rich buyer of horses and mules, Ballew befriended James Golden's family. They invited him to live with them, and he stayed several months.

Ballew eventually induced James Golden's father to loan him several thousand dollars for a business venture in Texas and persuaded James to go along with him.

"Ballew and James left the Golden house with a horse and wagon and a large trunk, on the expedition which was to bring fortune to the family," according to one account.

The pair traveled to Collin County, where Ballew ostensibly planned to sell the livestock. While camped about three miles outside of McKinney, as James prepared breakfast over a campfire, Ballew slipped behind him and slammed an axe into his skull. He buried Golden in a shallow grave and went on to McKinney. There Ballew wrote a letter to the Golden family, reassuring them of their progress and that he and Golden were headed back to Illinois.

But Ballew returned to Illinois without his traveling companion and claimed he didn't know what had happened to James. His stories didn't add up. And the family noticed a change in his behavior. As the older Mr. Golden testified:

> *Whenever my absent son's name was mentioned he would always let on he had taken a chill; seemed very nervous and excited whenever my son was mentioned; always wanted a light in his room at night; said he could not rest without a light in his room; would get up in the night and walk the floor and smoke. Before Ballew left with my son, he could rest as well as any of the family.*

This went on for months. Ballew claimed he'd hired an investigator to look for James. But the elder Golden finally became suspicious and had the authorities arrest Ballew. Sheriff Bush traveled to Illinois to bring Ballew back to Texas; while he was in custody, Golden's body was found buried in a shallow grave.

The trial that followed was so sensational that it was moved to the First Christian Church in McKinney because Collin County's courthouse couldn't hold all the spectators.[16] The prosecuting attorney noted the cruelty of Ballew's crime toward the family. "Because the family had been friends, tried and true, to this prisoner when he was left an orphan, friendless and homeless, we find them today grieving over their murdered son and brother—a distracted and miserable family," he said.

James Golden's skull and bones, along with the clothing found with the remains, were presented to the elder Mr. Golden in the courtroom, who identified them as those of his son.

Later, a contemporary account of the crime tried to find an explanation for Ballew's cruel crimes. The writer noted that Ballew's mother died when he was six, and he'd been inadequately supervised after that. He also surmised that lurid entertainment may have inspired his criminal nature. "He was fond of reading exciting tales, such as the daring deeds of desperadoes, remarkable trials and confessions, and everything of that character that fell into his hands he would peruse with the utmost avidity to the exclusion of everything else," the author wrote.

Stephen Ballew was found guilty and sentenced to be hanged from a tree in Finch Park on May 24, 1872. A large crowd—most of Collin County, according to newspaper reports—gathered for the execution.

Fifty years later, the *McKinney Courier-Gazette* published the reminisces of one Uncle Josh Herndon, an eyewitness to the hanging. He recalled that on the morning of the execution, Ballew ate a hearty breakfast, rode to the gallows on his coffin and smoked a cigar. He wore a nice suit of clothes and a big white hat. After mounting the gallows, Ballew took off his hat and handed it to Sheriff Bush, saying, "Here Captain, lay my hat over there."

"He then went to his death with all the nerve a man could," Herndon said.

Only one person in the crowd was there to mourn the death of Stephen Ballew—Clara, one of James Golden's younger sisters, who had married Ballew after he returned from Texas.

After the hanging, as the Plano men headed home, a terrible thunderstorm broke out. Accounts described it as one of the worst they'd ever seen, with hailstones so large they killed baby calves out on the prairie.

On that last violent note, the terrible tale of Stephen Ballew came to an end.

V

Haunted History

24
Death in Early Plano

Today, Americans fear getting old. In the nineteenth century, getting old was a privilege afforded only a few—and death was an accepted part of daily life.

"Dying—like being born—was generally a family, communal and religious event, not a medical one," according to a report, *A Profile of Death and Dying in America*. "Because many deaths occurred at home, people were likely to care for a dying relative and thus, to have a fairly personal and direct experience of death."[17]

Death was always near at hand in the nineteenth century. The average life expectancy at birth was fewer than fifty years in 1900; today, the typical American can expect to live a lengthy life and die at an old age. Infant and child mortality were almost routine—for every 1,000 babies born in 1900, more than 162 didn't see their first birthday.

Even those who made it to adulthood were much more likely to die of communicable disease. Influenza, tuberculosis and diphtheria were the biggest killers; heart disease, stroke and cancer ranked fourth, fifth and ninth. (Today, the latter three are the leading causes of death for older people.) Death often occurred suddenly and unexpectedly.

As a result, "Grief was more than just an emotion for Americans…it was a way of life," according to a National Museum of Funeral History (NMFH) essay on nineteenth-century mourning. "Victorian social etiquette put great social pressure on mourning, resulting in the practice of public mourning rather than private grieving."

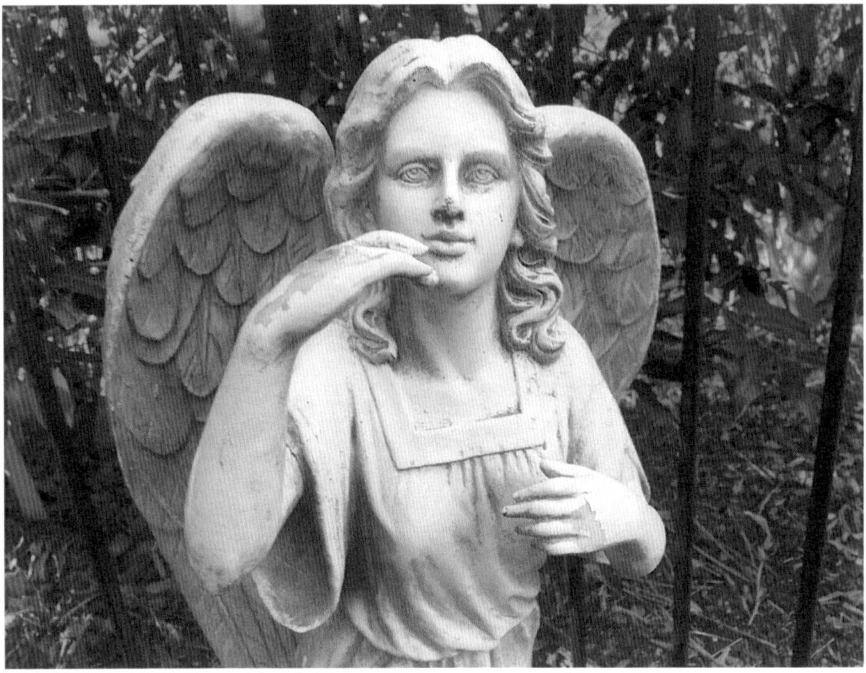

Angel in Collinsworth Cemetery. *Photo by the author.*

When someone died, family members usually handled everything that followed—digging the grave, preparing a shroud, laying out and dressing the dead. The body was kept at home. Neighbors pitched in, making sure that several people were present at all times while the body was laid out.

This vigil was an act of respect and courtesy as well as a way to make sure that varmints, especially cats, did not disturb the body. It was also a way of making certain that the deceased was really dead. Without modern medical technology, determining whether someone was truly dead was not as foolproof as it is today.

"During the days following a person's death, the body was closely observed for three days to make sure the person didn't wake from a deep sleep or illness before the funeral and burial," the NMFH website said. "Thus, the term 'wake' we use today for visiting or viewing the recently deceased."

When a family member died in early Plano, one of the family's first chores was to have black-bordered funeral announcements printed and delivered to local businesses. That allowed word to travel fast to friends and neighbors, who would then call at the home and make plans to attend the service.

There was no embalming, so the body was laid out on a board in the living room or parlor. If the weather was hot, a cool cloth was laid over the face and changed every half hour.

The casket remained open during the funeral, and the entire congregation would file past to pay last respects. The family remained at the burial site until the entire grave was filled in. "Many a time the sobs of the bereaved would mingle with the thuds of dirt falling on the coffin," according to *Plano, Texas: The Early Years.*

Neighbors shared the burden of caring for the dead and for the grieving family in early Plano. The diary of Elizabeth Carpenter tells of stopping her chores to pink the lining of a neighbor's coffin. For a span of about fifty years, the Rasor family dug most of the graves in Rowlett Cemetery, and the women of the family prepared food and flowers to take to the home of each grieving family. The family viewed this as their contribution to the community.

During the flu epidemic of 1918, this communal system was strained, as many died and others were too sick to perform funeral duties. When a death occurred, residents did the best they could. Someone would get a

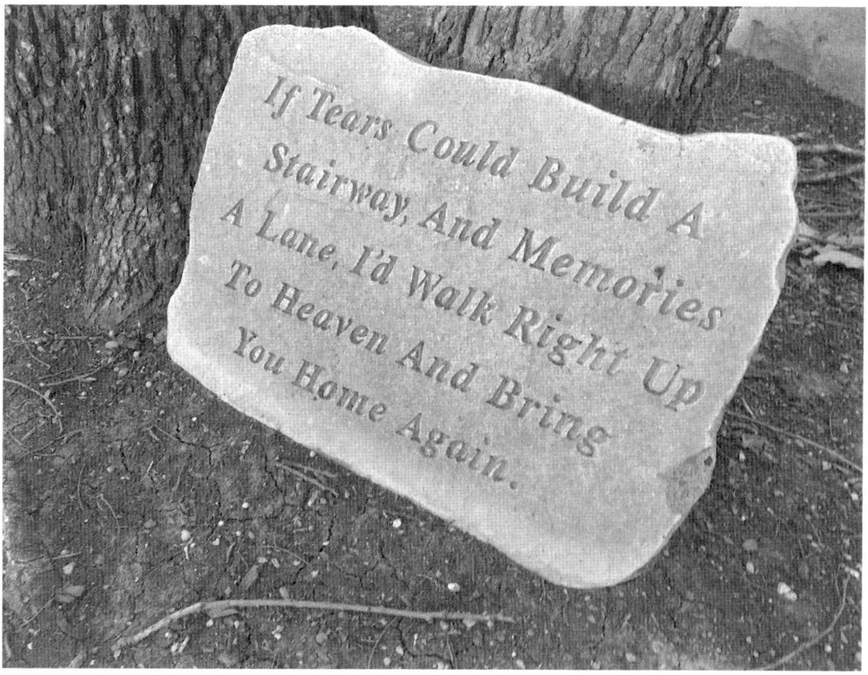

Plaque in Collinsworth Cemetery. *Photo by the author.*

coffin, somebody would find a wagon, a grave would be dug. "Very few people were up and going, and sometimes whole families were stricken," according to *Plano, Texas: The Early Years*. One family lost seven people during that epidemic.

With the arrival of the twentieth century, undertakers gradually took over many of the chores related to funerals. That's when parlors became known as "living rooms"—because they were no longer used to display the dead.

25

Keepers of the Family Plots

They are Plano's silent citizens—more than six thousand strong, residing quietly in out-of-the-way corners of our city. They are the departed souls of Plano's past, buried in about a dozen pioneer cemeteries around the city.

But these cemeteries are more than final resting places. With the earliest dating back to 1847, they are treasure-troves of stories and priceless bits of history. And they're open to all to enjoy, thanks to the efforts of a passionate group of Plano citizens who are still very much alive.

In the older cities in the eastern part of the United States, you'll find one or two large cemeteries situated near the center of town. By contrast, Plano's cemeteries are scattered.

Most of Plano's early residents lived on farms far from the town, and they had to bury their dead quickly—there was no embalming and no refrigeration. As a result, they buried family members on their own land or perhaps on the land of an adjacent neighbor.

Plano Mutual Cemetery, near downtown, is home to more than four thousand souls. But many of the other pioneer cemeteries in Plano are essentially tiny family plots. Most are no longer active—that is, they're no longer accepting new people for burial—but they are preserved and maintained with care.

"They're like a history book of our town," says Jeff Campbell, executive director of the Plano Conservancy for Historic Preservation. "Walking through these cemeteries, you can learn so much about Plano and its history."

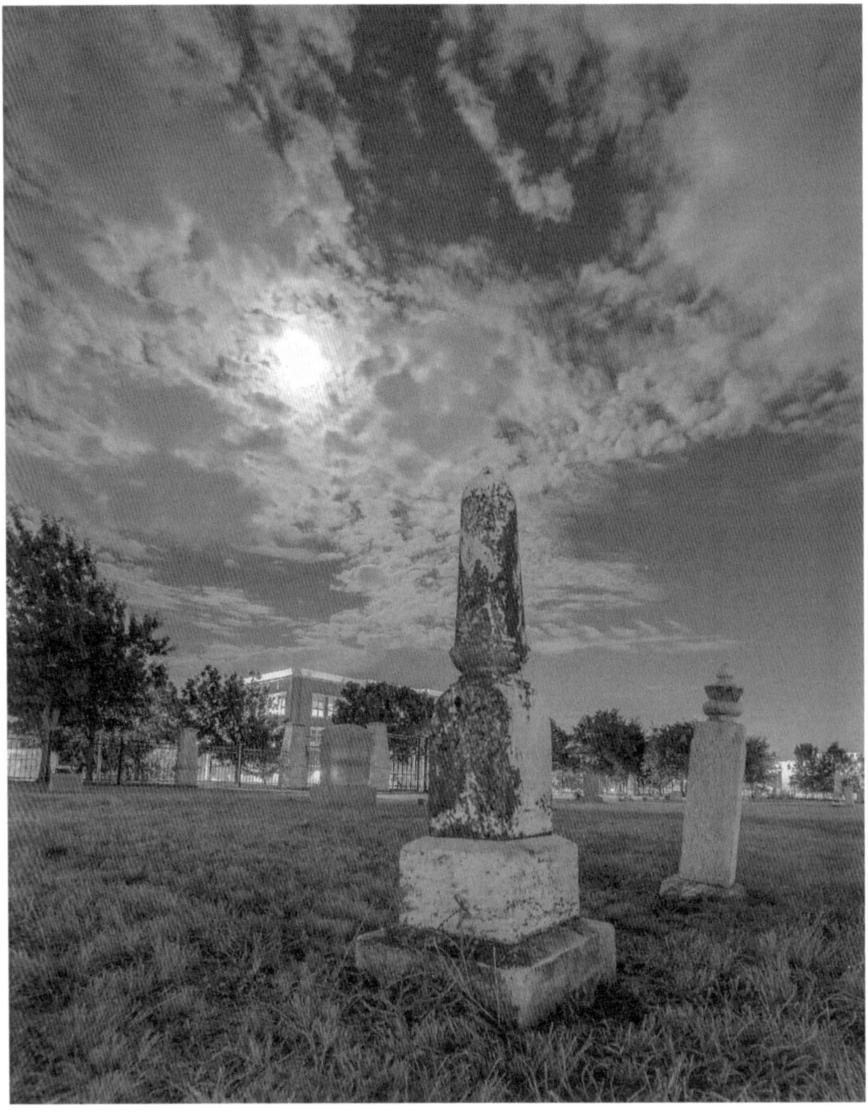

Baccus Cemetery, located in the heart of the Legacy Town Center. *Photo by David Downs.*

Many of these pioneer cemeteries are tucked in hidden corners of the city; others are more visible, like Baccus Cemetery, situated in the middle of the Shops of Legacy. There's Old City Cemetery, started by five of Plano's founders, and next to that, there's Davis Cemetery, a predominately African American cemetery.

Dedicated Volunteers

Plano residents can enjoy these cemeteries and their many treasures, thanks to the dedication and efforts of passionate volunteers like Joy Gough. They spend hours cleaning up cemeteries, sprucing them up with flowers, researching the history and the genealogy of those buried in them. Joy helped apply for markers that designate the cemeteries and protect them from being plowed under for development. Her work has been recognized with a Living Legacy award from the Collin County Historical Commission.

Many different volunteers and groups have donated countless volunteer hours to keep Plano's cemeteries in good shape. Inmates do cleanup work as part of a program through the Collin County Sheriff's Department. Scout troops, master gardeners, developers and descendants of the pioneer families have also pitched in.

Since most of these volunteers aren't descendants of the people buried in the cemeteries, what inspires them to spend hours and days maintaining Plano's family plots?

"The cemeteries are like outdoor art," said Candace Fountoulakis, a Plano resident and preservation advocate. "I love the beauty and poetry of the headstones. You can see how much their loved ones appreciated the people they lost."

Candace is especially moved by a series of small, heart-shaped headstones at Bethany Cemetery—all from one family that lost many children. "I don't think you could look at them without crying….It makes you realize the massive losses that many pioneers faced."

Other volunteers feel a deep connection to the folks buried in the pioneer cemeteries.

"When I'm working at a cemetery, I say a prayer," said Kenny Bush, a longtime resident and preservation advocate. "I talk to them. I'm taking care of their resting place. I fight those battles to keep the cemeteries, because they can't. It's a duty."

"It's a way for Plano people to embrace this history," said Jeff Campbell. "People built this city; it didn't just fall out of the sky. It's a way to tie the present to the past."

Candace adds that spending time in a cemetery—whether planting flowers, cleaning tombstones or just taking a moment to reflect—is a reminder of our mortality.

"It's serious and yet it's a beautiful place to be," she said. "It reminds you to make the best use of your time."

If you do visit one or more of Plano's cemeteries, be sure to follow proper cemetery etiquette. Visit only during daylight hours. Don't pick the flowers, and don't move anything, not even a random stone. Don't pick up anything except trash or, for the cemeteries near golf courses, perhaps a golf ball.

But be warned: the cemeteries may not be haunted with apparitions, but once the "cemetery bug" bites, it's easy to get hooked. Inevitably, uncovering the history of one tombstone leads to more mysteries; researching one family name or one historic event opens up questions that lead to more research.

"Once you get interested, you don't sleep at night," said Kenny. "You gotta have that answer."

26
TOMBSTONE MYSTERIES

In the rural South, families gather annually for Decoration Day—a combination reunion and workday, when family members clean up their privately owned graveyards and honor the memories of ancestors.

The Plano Conservancy has created its own version of Decoration Day: an annual event called Tombstone Mysteries. Hundreds of volunteers of all ages—virtually all of them unrelated to the cemetery's inhabitants—turn up to spruce up Plano's cemeteries. Participants learn how to clean tombstones, leave flowers at the tombs of veterans and take part in a scavenger hunt where they locate graves of historic significance and learn about Plano history.

TOMBSTONE TRIVIA

In the spirit of Tombstone Mysteries, here are some interesting tidbits and trivia about Plano's graveyards and the characters that inhabit them:

At Young Cemetery, a small graveyard hidden behind an apartment complex at 121 and Independence, you'll find the grave of Thomas Finley, who fought in the War of 1812, making him one of Plano's oldest veterans. You might also notice that a number of the headstones are identical—that's because they were likely purchased by mail-order from a Sears catalogue. (At one time, the catalogue offered dozens of pages of monuments of all types.)

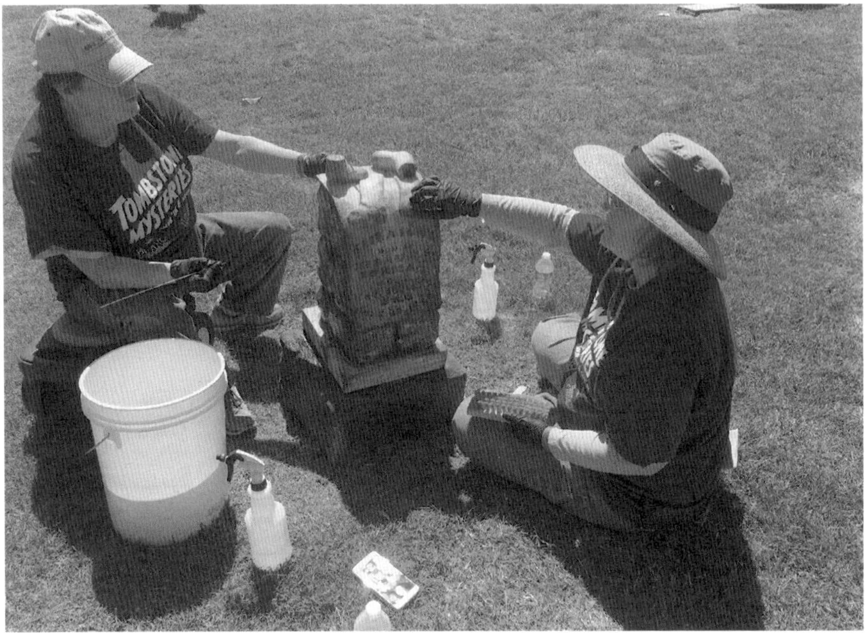

Participants in Tombstone Mysteries clean a grave at Plano Mutual Cemetery in 2017. *Photo by the author.*

In many Plano cemeteries, you'll spot tall, elaborately carved tombstones that look like tree trunks. Those are Woodmen of the World markers. Woodmen of the World Life Insurance Society, a not-for-profit fraternal benefit society, still operates out of Omaha. (If you saw the movie *About Schmidt*, Jack Nicholson plays a retired Woodman actuary.) Until 1930, the organization provided members with distinctive tombstones shaped like tree stumps. The headstones featured Woodmen relics and symbols: a stump or felled tree, the maul and wedge, an axe and often a dove of peace with an olive branch. As Woodmen "do not lie," a common inscription is "Here rests a Woodman of the World."

Headstones often provide a wealth of clues into the person buried underneath. At Plano Mutual, you'll see the ornate tomb of John Fouche (1848–1894), a Plano businessman. The headstone features a draped urn, an ancient symbol of death and mortality, with the draping representing the passage "through the veil" between one existence to another. Below the urn is a cluster of ivy, symbolizing eternity, fidelity and a strong bond of affection, such as a marriage or friendship. There are also symbols indicating Fouche's affiliation with the Knights of Pythias, a fraternal order.

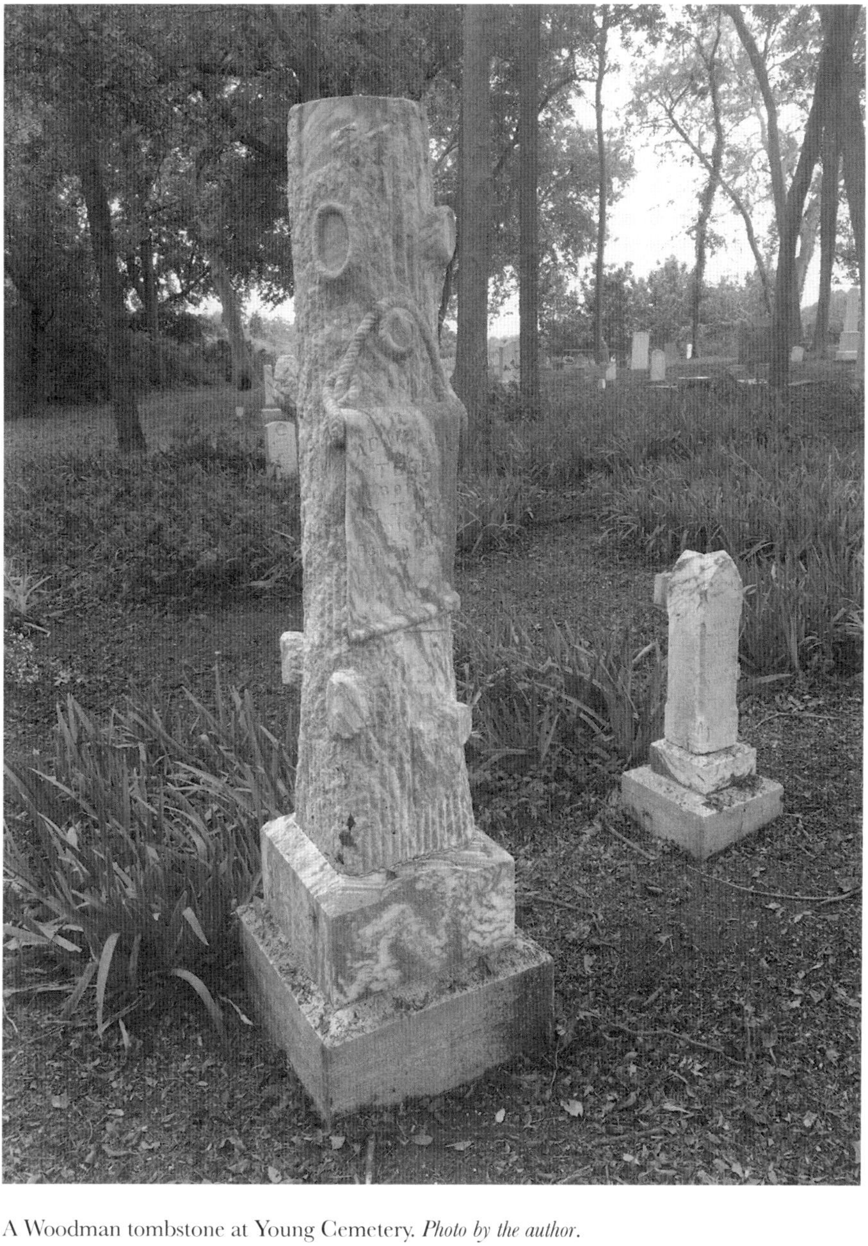

A Woodman tombstone at Young Cemetery. *Photo by the author.*

Other headstones reveal some of the threats that early residents faced. The Ross family was plagued by a series of violent deaths: John T. Ross (1919–1941) died in a farm accident after his head was crushed between two trucks; Ransom Ross (1847–1909) was killed by his daughter, the aptly named Belle Pistole, who allegedly shot him in a dispute over a child; and Richard Ross (1922–1943) was killed in an airplane during a training exercise in World War II.

TO LEARN MORE:

These are just a few examples of the colorful history waiting to be discovered at Plano's cemeteries. To check them out yourself, stop at the Interurban Railway Museum downtown and pick up a free brochure, *Driving Tour of Historic Plano Cemeteries.* The Interurban also offers *Plano's Historic Cemeteries* (Arcadia Publishing, 2014), by the Plano Conservancy for Historic Preservation Inc., for sale.

27
HALLOWEEN HIJINKS

In 2016, Plano made the "Top Ten" list in WalletHub's tally of Best Cities for Halloween. The rating was based on eighteen key indicators, including the number of costume stores per capita and a typical Halloween weather forecast. With high marks for good weather, low crime and "trick-or-treater friendliness," Plano ranked no. 8.

But those who grew up in Plano might argue that Plano's best Halloween years took place when Plano was still a small town.

Old houses—some of them abandoned or ramshackle—dotted the community, and those made for spooky Halloween speculation. In the 1970s, the Jaycees would transform the old George House into a haunted house. (The George House was located at Avenue L and Sixteenth Street and built in 1900; now it's at Old City Park in Dallas.)

Elementary schools hosted Halloween festivals, with games, prizes and treats. Everybody dressed up, including the teachers. Black-lit "haunted houses" thrilled kids with the chance to don blindfolds and feel "brains" (spaghetti) and "eyeballs" (peeled grapes.)

Many who grew up in Plano fondly recall trick-or-treating during a time when free-range parenting was the norm. Kids would run from house to house, toting pillowcases, hurrying so as to maximize their candy intake. Sometimes they'd swing by home, empty their pillowcases and head back out for more.

Kemper Smith remembered ladies who passed out homemade brownies and homemade popcorn balls from their homes. "People don't seem to give

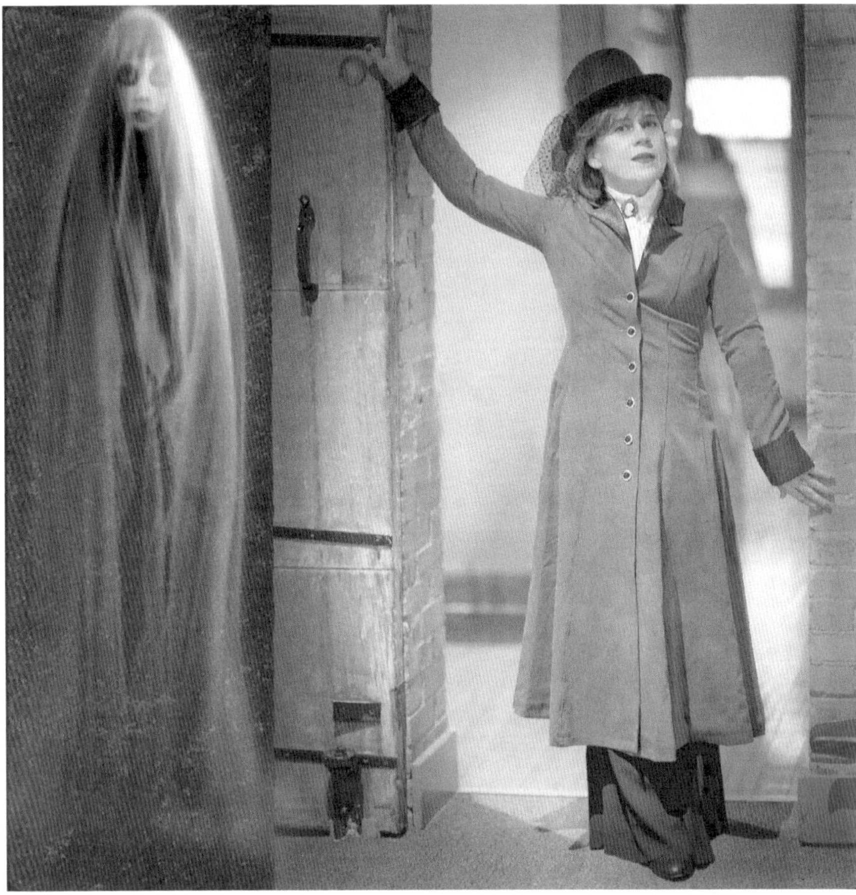

Above: Kathy Strobel (*right*), a guide at Apparition Expedition 2017, and an unidentified phantom. *Photo by Debi Adams.*

Opposite: The steps of the Carpenter House, Halloween 2017. *Photo by Debi Adams.*

homemade goodies anymore," he said. "Today's children don't know what they are missing."

Many remembered trick-or-treating at the sprawling and luxurious eastside home of Dollie Hasford, also known as "the Rich Lady," who passed out Hershey bars, sometimes along with a quarter. Word got out, and her home became a must-stop for every Plano child.

"We were in awe of those full-size candy bars," one resident recalled.

And then of course there were the pranks.

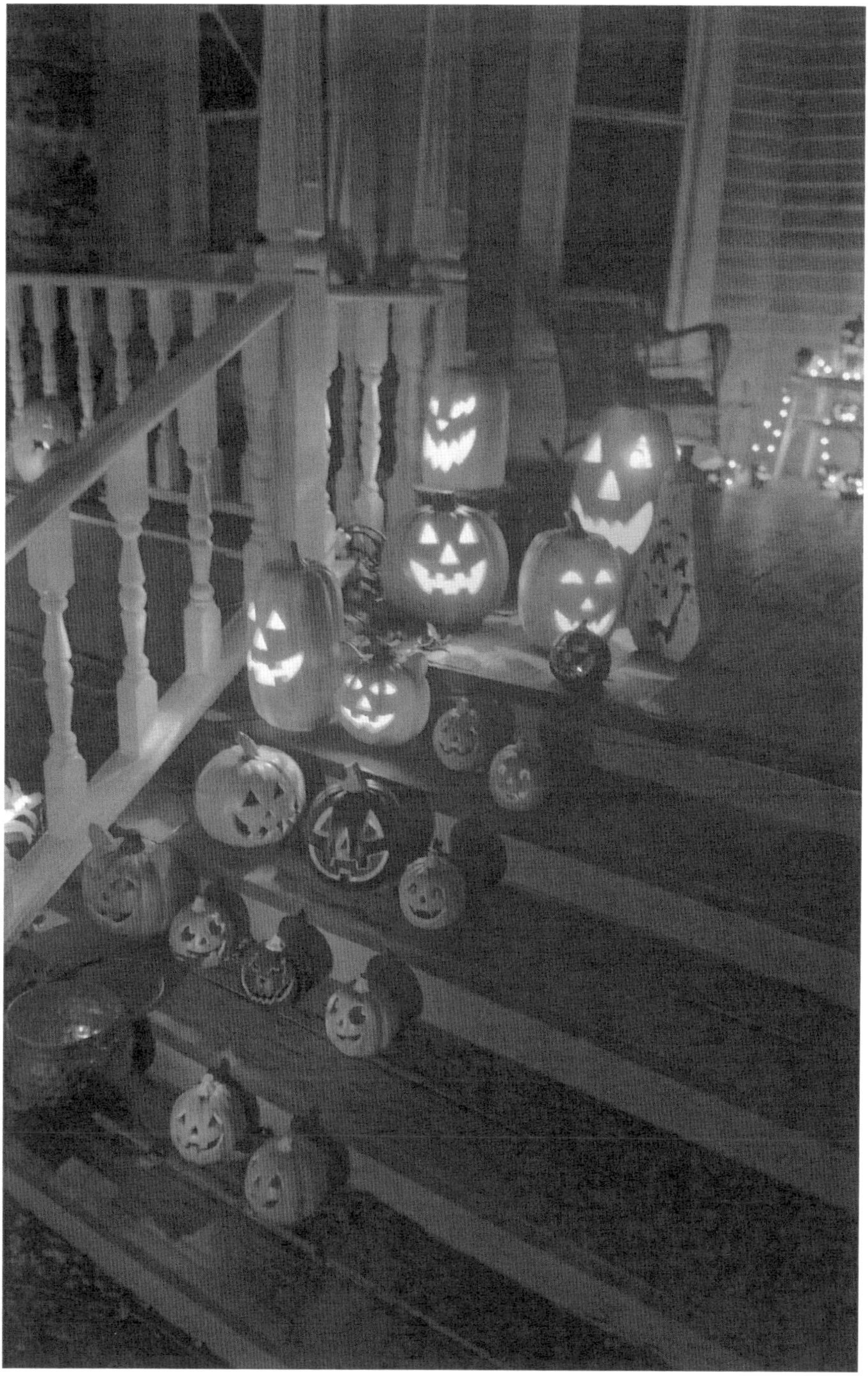

One resident remembered a Halloween night in the late 1940s, when a group of high school boys thought it might be funny to deposit an old wooden outhouse on the lawn of E.A. Sigler, the school superintendent.

"We all thought this was the height of hilarity!" she recalled.

But the all-time champions of Halloween hijinks in Plano would be the Twenty Tuff Tamales, a group of teen boys who hung out together in the 1920s.

Once, the Tamales hung a large porch swing, complete with chains, from the middle of the telephone wires on the north side of Mechanic Street, between the interurban rail and the Magnolia Gas Station. The porch swing remained there for weeks while the local officials tried to figure out how to get it down.

Another Halloween, the young ruffians managed to lead a cow to the top of the spiral staircase at the old school, and somehow, a wagon appeared on top of the Houston and Texas Central Depot building on the south side of Mechanic Street.

Despite the "tough" image they carefully cultivated, the Twenty Tuff Tamales quietly performed many good deeds. They would watch over the gas stations for one of the town's night guards while he slept on a bench.

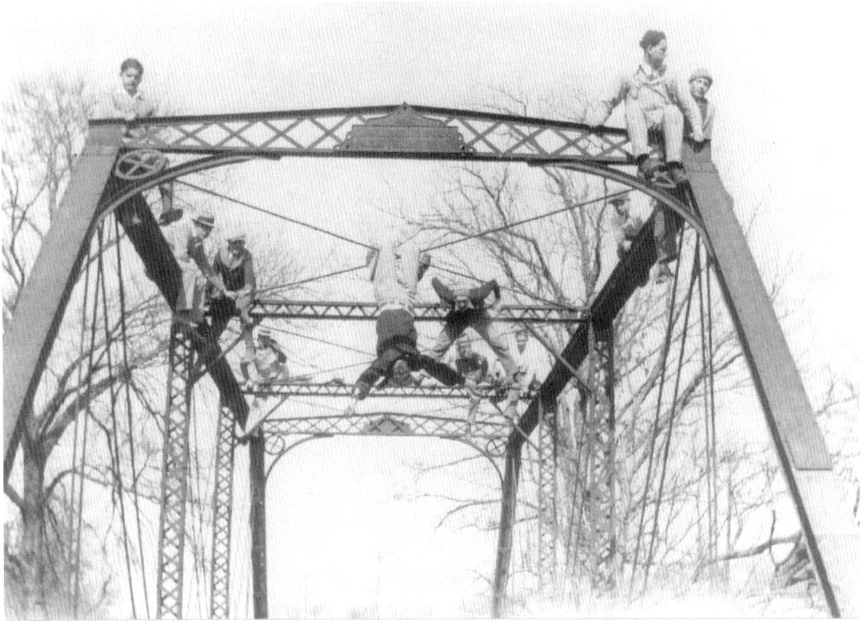

During the 1920s, the Twenty Tuff Tamales pulled off some ingenious Halloween pranks. *Courtesy of the Genealogy Center of the Plano Public Library.*

They were summoned by the telephone operator one time to help when a local man had been knocked down by a bull in his pasture.

The Heritage Farmstead shared this history a few years ago as part of an exhibit about the group:

> *The Twenty Tuff Tamales (TTT) club started in the late 1920s with a suggestion by Bert Carpenter, Sr. His three oldest sons, Willie, Buddy, and Elzie were close in age and, as a way to keep them off the streets and out of trouble, Mr. Carpenter encouraged the boys to form a club. They invited their friends to join and called themselves the "Ten Tuff Tamales," a name inspired by a comic strip carried in the* Plano Star Courier. *Membership of the club was eventually expanded to twelve and finally twenty boys; the numbers had to start with "T" so the initials TTT could be preserved.*
>
> *In order to conduct their meetings and plan activities, the TTT's needed a clubhouse. The boys took over Bert Carpenter, Sr.'s small house he built behind the family home on 16th Street in downtown Plano and named it, "the shack." The shack had a wood burning stove, game tables, two beds that could sleep 6 to 8 boys, and plenty of quilts for latecomers to use for sleeping on the floor. It was considered a real honor to even be allowed to enter the "shack."*
>
> *The TTT's took their club very serious. They conducted regular meetings the second Sunday of the month, paid dues, and recorded minutes. The TTT's chose the poison warning label symbol of the skull and crossbones as their emblem to imply the group was "so tough they were as dangerous as poison." Each member had a special lapel pin with blue TTT letters encased on a silver background, a belt buckle with the skull and crossbones emblem, and black sweaters with an orange emblem of the skull and crossbones on the front and TTT written on the back.*
>
> *The club did get into trouble once with the radio stations WFAA and WBAP, who were the only local stations at the time. The boys had built a crystal set to send and receive Morse Code. However, their messages were unintentionally interfering with the public broadcasts. The Carpenter family was visited by a representative of the U.S. government who asked the boys to stop.*

28
What Lurks Beneath

There's something inherently sinister about old water wells. If you've ever seen the movie *The Ring*, it's not hard to imagine them as watery portals to the underworld.

Maybe that's why people are fascinated when they learn that many old buildings in Plano still have wells—Holman House, Carpenter House and XO Coffee, to name a few. For a time, Plano was known as the City of Wells because wells were the only source of water. Downtown wells were dug in part to help fight fires after several conflagrations destroyed buildings downtown in the late nineteenth century.

The Old Community Well, an office space and event venue at 1029 East Fifteenth Street, draws its name from the well that's right in the middle of its ground floor. That well was likely dug around 1885, according to old maps of the area. Like most of Plano's old wells, it was sealed shut—until October 2017.

Proprietor Mason Ice had the well's steel grate cut open for the first time in more than fifty years. While attendees of the Apparition Expedition ghost tour watched, he lowered a Go Pro camera down the well and shared the images via Facebook Live.

Similar explorations of other downtown wells in recent years have turned up vintage items, like old bottles and tools. Unfortunately, Mason's efforts only brought up a "a very historic roll of masking tape." But he plans to try again, next time with better extraction tools.

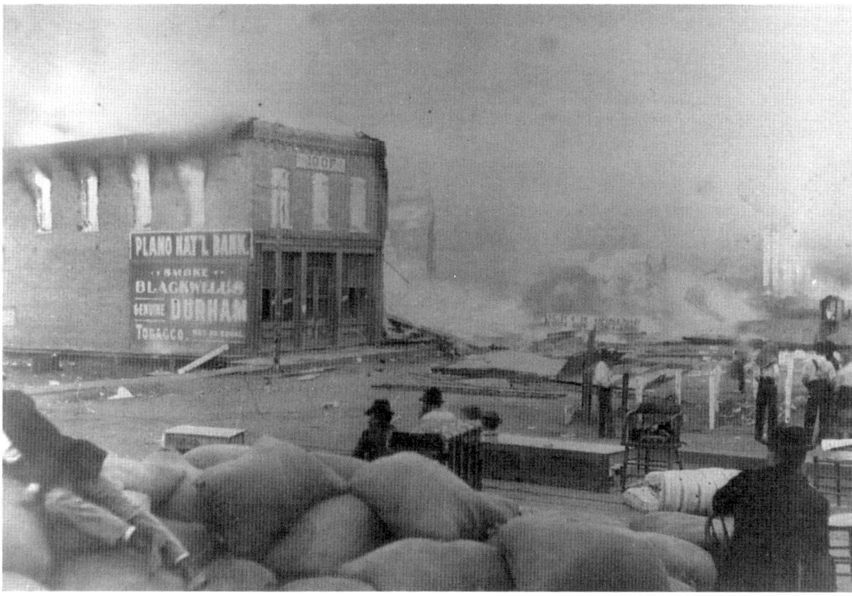

A series of fires destroyed many buildings in downtown Plano in the late nineteenth century. *Courtesy of the Genealogy Center of the Plano Public Library.*

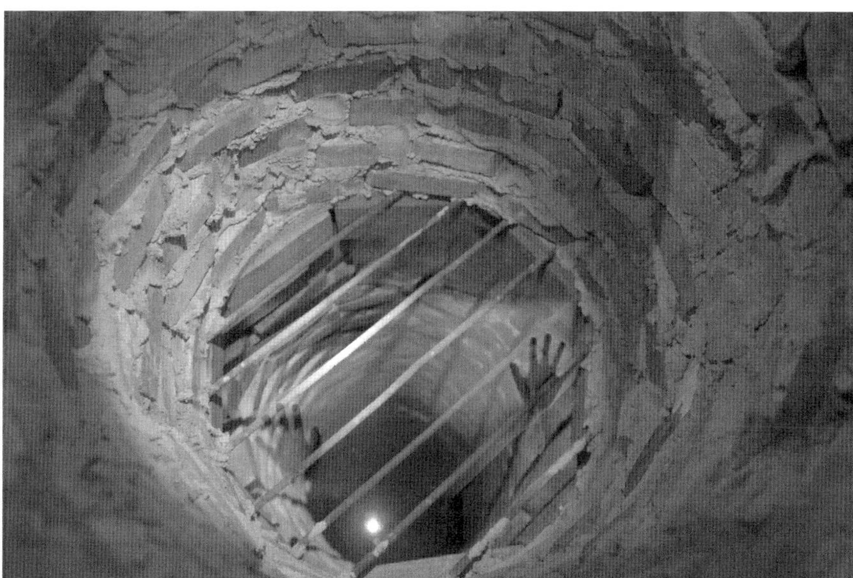

The Old Community Well was opened for the first time in fifty years for Apparition Expedition 2017. *Photo by Debi Adams.*

Notes

I. The Haunted City

1. "Cruising Historical Collin County," brochure published by the Collin County Historical Commission.
2. Friends of the Plano Public Library, *Plano, Texas: The Early Years* (Wolfe City, TX: Henington Publishing Company, 1996), 5.
3. "Cruising Historical Collin County."

II. Ghost Sightings

4. *Plano, Texas*, 41.
5. "Ten Haunted Day Trips in Texas that Will Make You Tremble with Fear," Backpackerverse, https://backpackerverse.com/day-trips-in-texas/#7_Heritage_Farmstead_Museum_Plano.
6. Hillary Kidd and Jessica Bell, *Never A Good Girl: The Renegade Spirit of the Farrell-Wilson Family* (Virginia Beach, VA: Donning Company Publishers, 2013).
7. Brenda Kellow, "Early Mass Transit in Plano," Star Local Media, http://StarLocalMedia.com/opinion/blogs/blog_7.
8. Stacy S. Wykie, "The Public Will vs. The Public Trust: Early American Radio as a Public Information Resource," MSIS, Graduate School of

Library and Information Science, University of Illinois at Urbana–Champaign. Presented at the 79th ASIS&T Annual Meeting, October 14–18, 2016, in Copenhagen, Denmark.

III. Urban Legends

9. *Plano, Texas*, 295–96.
10. "Man Says He Had Encounter with Scary Clown in Plano," WFAA-TV, October 3, 2016, http://www.wfaa.com/news/local/collin-county/man-says-he-had-encounter-with-scary-clown-in-plano-last-week/328773377.
11. Melissa Chan, "Everything You Need to Know About the 'Clown Attack' Craze," *Time*, October 4, 2016, http://time.com/4518456/scary-clown-sighting-attack-craze.
12. "Are Creepy Clowns Really a Threat?" *USA Today*, October 5, 2016, https://www.usatoday.com/story/news/nation-now/2016/10/05/creepy-clowns-really-threat/91613506.

IV. Dark Moments in Plano History

13. Donald R. Hopkins, MD, MPH, "Smallpox: Ten Years Gone," *American Journal of Public Health* (December 1988).
14. "The Child Whose Town Rejected Vaccines," Wellcome Collection, July 13, 2017, wellcomecollection.org.
15. J.H. Dudley, "The Climax in Crime of the Nineteenth Century, Being an Authentic History of the Trial, Conviction and Execution of Stephen Merris Ballew, for the Murder of James P. Golden, in Collin County, Texas, on the 21st day of October, 1870, with a Short Sketch of the Early Life of the Murderer," in John Davison Lawson and Robert Lorenzo Howard, *American State Trials: A Collection of the Important and Interesting* (Google Books, 1917), https://archive.org/stream/americanstatetr08howagoog/americanstatetr08howagoog_djvu.txt.
16. Lawson and Howard, *American State Trials*. Transcript and contemporary account of the trial of Stephen Ballew can be found here, https://archive.org/stream/americanstatetr08howagoog/americanstatetr08howagoog_djvu.txt.

V. HAUNTED HISTORY

17. M.J. Field and C.K. Cassel, eds., Institute of Medicine (U.S.) Committee on Care at the End of Life, *Approaching Death: Improving Care at the End of Life* (Washington, D.C.: National Academies Press 1997), available from https://www.ncbi.nlm.nih.gov/books/NBK233601.

About the Author

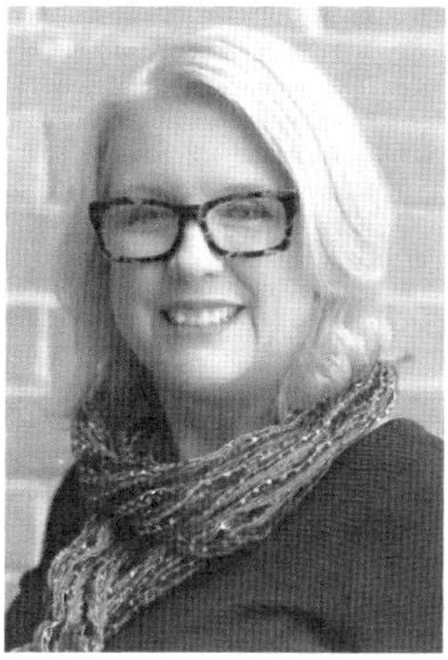

Courtesy of the City of Plano.

Mary Jacobs is producer of *Plano Podcast* and a freelance writer specializing in health and fitness, spirituality and issues relating to older adults. She writes regularly for the *Dallas Morning News*, The Silver Century, Religion News Service, United Methodist News Service and other outlets. Mary was a founding organizer of TEDxPlano in 2014 and served as a speaker in 2017. Mary and her husband, Steve Lavine, have four grown children and live in Plano, Texas, in a home ruled by a five-pound Yorkie.